S0-AGT-968

THE NEW
Chihuahua

THE NEW
Chihuahua

E. Ruth Terry

HOWELL
BOOK HOUSE
New York

Howell Book House
Macmillan General Reference
A Simon & Schuster Macmillan Company
15 Columbus Circle
New York, NY 10023

Copyright © 1990 by Howell Book House

All rights reserved. No part of this book may be reproduced or
transmitted in any form or by any means, electronic or mechanical,
including photocopying, recording, or by any information storage
and retrieval system, without permission in writing from the
Publisher.

Library of Congress Cataloging-in-Publication Data

Terry, E. Ruth, 1927-
    The new Chihuahua/by E. Ruth Terry.
        p.   cm.
    Bibliography: p.
    ISBN 0-87605-125-5
    1. Chihuahua dogs.   I. Title.
SF429.C45T47 1990   89-11140   CIP
636.7'6—dc20

10 9 8 7 6

Printed in the United States of America

To my family
for their help and support
in the preparation of this work

About the Author

FROM EARLY CHILDHOOD, E. Ruth Terry's interest in animals, dogs in particular, was of great importance.

Terrymont Kennels, Reg. was created in 1957 and is jointly owned with her husband, Herbert. Although they have a very limited breeding program, Terrymont has produced many champions, particularly Long Coat Chihuahuas. Most of these also hold obedience titles.

As they were growing up, the Terry children, Susan and Brian, were very active in conformation classes, obedience training and Junior Showmanship.

Mrs. Terry obtained her B.S. in Education from the Massachusetts School of Art and continued with graduate studies at Boston University. Her art background and interest in dogs have been combined through a career as a portrait painter, with emphasis on animal subjects.

Since 1969, her activity in dog show judging, which includes the Toy group plus many other breeds, has added to her participation in the sport of dogs.

Mrs. Terry is also an accomplished amateur musician on the guitar, banjo and synthesizer.

Contents

THE NEW
Chihuahua

Replicas of ancient clay figures, possibly Mayan or Aztec, sometimes referred to as the Dancing Chihuahuas. Some believe them to be Xoloitzcuintli.

1

The History of
the Chihuahua

THE ORIGIN of the Chihuahua is intertwined in history, folklore and legend, and in many instances is quite obscure and mysterious. There are several theories invoked as to how the breed came to be on this continent. With so many theories involved, it is difficult to separate fact from fiction. Many authorities write that the Chihuahua is originally from Mexico; others state that it began in Egypt, moving through various Mediterranean countries and on to Malta. Some people believe it originated in China, and a few researchers state the Chihuahua was bred from the Xoloitzcuintli (pronounced Show-low-itz-kwint-lee), a hairless native Mexican dog. There is even a theory that our Chihuahua's ancestors did not exist before the Spanish came to the New World, but that these same Spanish explorers were the first breeders of these little dogs.

Much of the Chihuahua's early history was recorded in languages other than English. Early works in Spanish contained many idiomatic phrases and were difficult to translate. Even those early works promoted various speculations about the Chihuahua, intertwining fact with fiction.

The most common and popular prevailing theories on the origin of the Chihuahua begin with the Mayans, Toltecs and Aztecs.

Little is known about the breed before the Mayan culture or what is thought of as ancient Mexico. Evidence found in archaeological digs bears little resemblance to our modern-day Chihuahua. As far as our Chihuahua is concerned, it is impossible to trace the breed to a recognizable ancestor before this period.

The Toltecs' history is rather obscure, but it is known that they existed in what is now Mexico in the ninth century and for several centuries thereafter. It is said that the Techichi, a small, long-haired dog of heavy bone that may have been mute, was part of the Toltec culture as early as the ninth century. This is supposedly the ancestor of the Chihuahua, according to some theorists.

Although there seems to be no established record of the Techichi before the ninth century, legend has it that the dog had ancestors as early as the fifth century, coinciding with the ruling Mayan tribes. The Toltec Techichi, however, is recorded in the stone carvings of a monastery of Franciscan monks of the early 1500s, known as the Monastery of Huejotzingo. Parts of the monastery were built of construction materials taken from the Pyramids of Cholula, which were of Toltec origin. It is these materials that contain the carvings depicting a small dog more recognizable as a Chihuahua as we know it today.

Many relics found in this region point to the existence of what may be Chihuahua ancestors in the area now known as Mexico City. There have been questions raised regarding actually finding ancestral specimens of the breed in the State of Chihuahua, the largest and northernmost state of Mexico and a mountainous region. An off-shoot version of Chihuahua beginnings has it that the Techichi was crossed with the wild Perro Chihuahueño, found in the region of the State of Chihuahua. Other historians have speculated that the Techichi was crossed with a small hairless dog brought over the Bering Strait from China to Alaska. This crossbreeding, it is said, helped to bring the Chihuahua down to a smaller size. However, there is little evidence of toy dogs existing in China in a period coinciding with the Toltec civilization.

The Toltecs were conquered by the Aztecs, and for several centuries, it is said, the small dogs continued to be the prized possessions of the rich. The peasants or commoners were either not interested in or could not afford to own and maintain the breed, and may only have used the small dog for human consumption.

The first evidence of a doglike animal bearing any resemblance to our present day Chihuahua is more likely to be from the era of

Replica of clay dog figure from Colima. It is more recognizable as a Xoloitzcuintli than as a Chihuahua.

Replica of a Tarascan pottery dog vessel from Colima. Some think this is a fat Chihuahua puppy; in reality, it more closely resembles the Xolo. This is a good example of how these breeds' histories intertwine.

the Aztecs, conquerors of the Toltecs. It is said that the Aztecs were fond of this little dog, and because remains were found in human graves, it is speculated that the breed had some religious significance. It is believed that the Aztecs used the little dogs as religious sacrifices, particularly when the owners died. The dogs were sacrificed and interred with the master's remains with the thought that the sins of the master were transferred to the dog's remains, thus not incurring the wrath of the gods and insuring safe passage of the master's soul from evil spirits and guiding it to its final destination or resting place. The Aztec culture lasted about 500 years, until the conquest of the Aztecs by Cortés and his men in the early sixteenth century. Little is known of the Chihuahua during that time. It is written that the little dogs became nearly extinct, as they were constantly used as meat to be eaten.

Records note that when Christopher Columbus landed in Cuba, he found a small, mute, tame dog. Whether or not these animals were of Chihuahua type is not known, other than from the description of their small size. Because the Aztecs were primarily land dwellers, it seems quite unlikely that they were responsible for the toy-sized dogs in Cuba.

From the time of the Spanish conquest, little is known of the Chihuahua until later in the nineteenth century. In tales repeated through the years, it is said that around the mid-1800s some Chihuahuas were found in the possession of certain peasants near what was said to be castle ruins of the last Aztec monarch, the emperor Montezuma, near Casas Grandes. Although it is questionable that this was actually a royal palace built in that remote northern part of the country, the dogs that were found with the peasants had the molera (a soft spot in the middle of the head), long nails and large ears of today's Chihuahuas. Thereafter, similar dogs were found in various other parts of the country.

Another version of the origin of our little Toy dog states that a breed resembling the Chihuahua came from Malta. The reasoning behind this theory is that these small, smooth-coated dogs possessed the molera, a characteristic for which the modern Chihuahua is noted. By the mid-seventeenth century little dogs of this type began to appear all over Europe, which is probably why small dogs resembling Chihuahuas appear in some paintings by the Old Masters of Europe.

Other fanciful tales concerning the Chihuahua persist today—one that the Chihuahua's warm body can be used as a hot water

A sketch from photographs of mounted Chihuahua specimens at the National Museum, Mexico City.

Terry

Present-day Xolo Ch. Xcels Aztec, which clearly shows that today this breed in no way resembles the Chihuahua. Bred by Janet Bidmead, owned by Terrymont Kennels, Herbert and E. Ruth Terry.

Another breed frequently confused with the Chihuahua is the Chinese Crested Dog, hairless variety. On the left is eleven-month-old Smooth Coat Chihuahua Razzmatazz Sweet William, with four-month-old Razzmatazz Rosebud, a Chinese Crested puppy, both owned by Amy Fernandez.

bottle to help such illnesses as stomachaches and arthritis, and another that the breed can be used as a deterrent for asthma sufferers. All this, of course, is quite fanciful, although even today there are many people who believe these stories to be true. Perhaps just believing helps to bring about relief from—or even cures of—various ailments.

There are those who disagree entirely with the aforementioned legends; they believe that all this folklore really describes the Xoloitzcuintle. The Xolo, as it is called for short, is sometimes called the Mexican Hairless and is now known as the national dog of Mexico.

The Xolo is frequently mistaken for the Chihuahua, or at least the smallest size is. There have even been some historians who have claimed that the Chihuahua is a direct descendant of the Xolo. This seems rather incredible, as about the only thing they have in common is that both seem to have Mexican origins. The legends associated with the Chihuahua are intertwined with Xolo folklore, which would make the theory of the Chihuahua as a descendant of the Xolo an unlikely one.

When the World Dog Show was held in Mexico City in 1978, a commemorative postage stamp was issued by the Mexican postal system in honor of the Xolo; depicted on the stamp is Pelona, an International and World Champion owned by Contessa Lascelles de Premio Réal of Mexico.

The Federacion Canofila Mexicana, A.C., affiliated with the Federation Cynologique Internationale, also known as the FCI, recognizes only two sizes for the hairless Xolo: the Miniature, shown in the Toy Group; and the Standard, which is in the Working Group. The breed under this Mexican standard ranges in size from 13 inches to 22.5 inches at the withers. The Xoloitzcuintli Club of America (note the slightly different spelling here), which as yet has no official AKC status, recognizes three sizes: Toy, in the Toy Group; Miniature, in the Non-Sporting Group; and Standard, in the Working Group. The FCI does not accept the coated variety; the XCA recognizes both hairless and coated varieties.

The legends and folklore, which are certainly varied and cover a very wide range of opinions, are interesting and fun to hear about, but in the long run it is up to the reader to decide which is which.

Ch. Hurd's Honey Bee won Best in Show at Cedar Rapids KC. Judge, Ed Bracy; handler, Peggy Hogg; breeder/owner, Max E. Hurd. Honey Bee was the top Chihuahua in 1969 and 1970, winning thirteen Toy Groups and thirty-eight placings in Groups. *Cedar Rapids Gazette*

2

The Chihuahua Comes to the United States

SOME OF THE FIRST small dogs resembling today's Chihuahuas were found along the Mexican, Arizona and Texas borders. In fact, they were called by interchangeable names such as "Mexican dogs," "Arizona dogs" and "Texas dogs." However, because some of these dogs purchased by Americans were bought in the State of Chihuahua from peasants living in that area, this was the name that became final and is retained to this day.

It was in the mid-1800s that American visitors to Mexico became enthralled with the tiny dogs and brought many specimens back to the United States, where the breed slowly became rather popular. In the spring of 1888, James Watson, a well-known dog authority, author and dog show judge of that time, brought some of these little dogs to the United States. He wrote of his purchase in two publications: in the May 1888 issue of the *American Kennel Register* and in March 1914, in *Country Life in America,* although the two articles differed somewhat in describing how the purchase actually came about. Watson's first dog was coated, and was a bitch he named Manzanita. During the next few years, Watson bought several more Chihuahuas along the border. He states, though, that the type varied considerably, not just in size and conformation but also in coat type and color. The dogs did have one thing in common, however, and that is that they all had the opening in the top of the skull known as the molera.

Clifford Hubbard, a noted English authority, had quite different thoughts regarding the origin of the breed. He believed that the Chihuahua was originally from Europe and was brought to Mexico after the Spanish conquest, perhaps crossing the Papillon with the Techichi. It is interesting to note that this may be a credible theory, for there are some European paintings that lend credence to Hubbard's beliefs, notably a painting by Botticelli. In the Sistine Chapel, circa 1482, Botticelli depicted the life of Moses, including a head study of a small, smooth dog with very long nails, large eyes and ears, remarkably like our Chihuahua today. Note the date: This was ten years before Columbus's landing in the New World!

Some people feel that the Long Coat Chihuahua was achieved by crossing the Chihuahua with the Pomeranian or with the Papillon, but most researchers insist that the long coat is truly a variety of the breed and they note that some of the first imports were Long Coats. In fact, it has been established that the earliest noted stud dog, Caranza, was a tiny Long Coat imported from Mexico by Owen Wister and Charles Stewart of Philadelphia. Records point to Caranza as being the progenitor of some of the leading strains in the early period of Chihuahuas in the United States. Caranza was listed as being a red Long Coat with ruby eyes, weighing three pounds. From Caranza came two strains, Meron and Perrito, well known for producing long coats.

In the late 1800s, interest in many breeds of dog arose. Kennel clubs were organized and dog shows began, sometimes in conjunction with livestock shows and sometimes alone. The *American Kennel Club Stud Book* of 1890 was the first to list Chihuahuas as having been exhibited in classes at dog shows. From 1890 onward, early growth of the breed was extremely slow, with just a few shown here and there. It is believed there were many Chihuahuas in existence, but very few were exhibited. Most were kept in homes as companions, and many of these were not registered. Even today, considering that thousands of Chihuahuas are registered each year with the AKC, proportionately few are exhibited.

The first Chihuahua registered in the 1904 AKC Stud Book was Midget, #2291, bred and owned by H. Rayner of El Paso, Texas. Midget was born on July 18, 1903; his sire was Pluto and his dam was Blanca, neither of which was registered. In the same Stud Book was Bonito, #2292, littermate to Midget. All five entries in the 1904

Ch. Hurd's Lil Indian. Breeder/owners, Max and Marie Hurd; handler, Clara Alford. At the CCA, 1964, he was Best of Winners under judge J. J. Duncan.
Alexander

Ch. Smithers' Angel Feathers, Southern California CC, Best of Breed, 1968, owner, Ruth Morrow; judge, Dr. Harold Huggins. Angel Feathers was an outstanding Long Coat of that period, ranking Number 1.

Stud Book were bred by H. Rayner, who retained ownership of four; the other was owned by J. M. Lee of Los Angeles.

In 1904 a mere 11 Chihuahuas were exhibited in the entire United States. Twelve years later, in 1916, only 50 were in competition. In 1962, 5,819 competed. The numbers have steadily increased through the years, with competition in 1987 equalling 14,758. Of these, 7,107 were Long Coats and 7,651 were Smooth Coats.

The first AKC championship awarded to a Chihuahua was earned by Beppie, Registration #85317, bred and owned by Mrs. L. A. McLean of Hackensack, New Jersey. Beppie, a white and fawn, was born February 2, 1903, and registered in 1905. Her sire was Bonito and her dam was Carlotta. Championships at that time, however, were based on the total number of animals from all breeds present, not on the number present from an individual breed.

It is important to mention some of the early strains of foundation stock of Chihuahuas in the United States. It is doubtful that any pure strain of the original Chihuahua bloodlines exists today. There are just too many breeders today who have outcrossed many times over into various other bloodlines to achieve the very best possible breeding potential for outstanding quality Chihuahuas. Early breeders and fanciers were also a dedicated lot, and although their kennel names are no longer on today's pedigrees, these people were truly responsible for the many wonderful Chihuahuas we have today. It is only through their devotion and love for the Chihuahua that we, as breeders today, are able to carry on with our dogs, bringing the breed to the popularity and state of excellence now enjoyed.

Here is a partial listing of early breeders and some of the kennel prefixes:

Mrs. C. D. Atwood
Evelyn Brush-Benner; Don Rubio; from the West Coast
Clara Dobbs
Ida H. Garrett
Olive C. Grudier; Don Apache
Sarah Holland; Don Sergio (chocolate and white Long Coats);
    Duxbury, Massachusetts
Mayme Cole Holmes-Grigsby; Perralto; Kansas
Mrs. L. A. McLean; New Jersey
Paul Mourman; Miniatura; New Orleans
Bertha Peaster; La Rex Doll; Philadelphia
Ann Radcliffe; founded the Meron strain (strong in Long Coats

Ch. Rayal's Cameo Keepsake, top winning Long Coat in 1970. Breeder/owner, Alberta "Pat" Booth. *Ludwig*

Ch. Komo's Tao Keno Reno was a Group placing dog shown by breeder/owner Katherine Hood. He earned many Best Veteran wins at Specialty shows. *Graham*

Ch. Terrymont Gospel John Ruff was Winners Dog at CC of Atlanta, under breeder/judge Carolyn Stober Hamilton. Breeder, Terrymont Kennels; owner, Ruth Morrow. *Ritter*

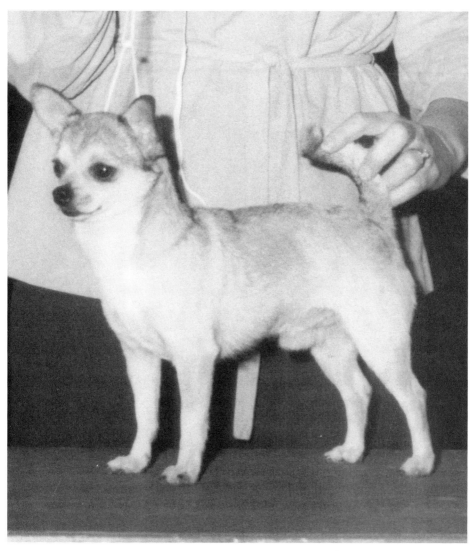

Ch. Hale's Bonanza Little Joe; breeder/owners Charles and Myrle Hale. He earned multiple Group placings and sired more than twenty-four champions. *Graham*

Ch. Gindon Bo-Jengles of Dartan. Best of Breed at CCA, October 1974. Breeder, Alice Page; owners, Darwin Delaney and J. Robert Laidley; judge, Maxwell Riddle. *Robert Holiday*

from the sire, Caranza) and was the first to register the Wister-Stewart dogs.

Edith Rhodes; Boo; Michigan

Charles Stewart and Owen Wister; owners of the famed Long Coat sire, Caranza; Philadelphia

Anna Vinyard; La Oro (also Si Si)

There was a well-known Perrito strain, but the last one in that line was registered in 1927.

The popularity of the Chihuahua increased, resulting in the founding of the Chihuahua Club of America in 1923 and the introduction of a Standard of Excellence for the breed. This standardization was a big step toward increasing the numbers of the breed in the United States. We see this illustrated by the fact that after the first registrations in the AKC Stud Book in 1904, for the next nineteen years only 170 were registered, with 38 becoming champions. In 1947, there were 40,526 Chihuahuas registered; in 1958, 45,843; in 1975, 16,494; and in 1987 there were 21,398 registered.

At the Philadelphia Kennel Club show held September 16 through 19, 1884, Chi Chigas, a Chihuahua-Terrier, was entered by William H. McCracken in the Miscellaneous/Foreign Dogs Class. One hundred years later, November 17 through 18, 1984, at the same Philadelphia Kennel Club event, there were 26 Smooth Coat Chihuahuas and 25 Long Coat Chihuahuas entered in the regular classes. There were also 5 Chihuahuas in the Obedience classes.

The Long Coat and the Smooth Coat were shown together until August 1, 1952, when they were separated into two varieties, for show classification purposes only. Revisions in the Standard by the Chihuahua Club of America were approved by the AKC on August 14, 1934, again on January 12, 1954, and once more in September 1972. It is possible that a revision may occur in the 1990s.

The first separately held Specialty Show occurred in 1946 with an entry of 71 and was judged by Forest N. Hall of Dallas, Texas. At the Chihuahua Club of America Specialty Show, held in Lincolnwood, Illinois, on October 7, 8, and 9, 1988, there was an entry of 113 Long Coats and 116 Smooth Coats in the regular classes, with a Puppy Sweepstakes entry of 39 Long Coats and 39 Smooth Coats. Some of the noted breeders present at this 1988 event had outstanding Chihuahuas as early as the 1940s, and have continued their winning ways right through the 1980s. Based on their early years, I would expect these high-quality breeding programs to continue for many years to come.

Ch. ELH's Mighty Lunar of Dartan was shown by co-owner Sheila Peters. At time of campaigning, he was co-owned with Elinor Hastings. Breeders, Darwin and Tanya Delaney. This dog had seven Bests in Show, thirty-eight Group Firsts and Best of Variety at Westminster 1983 and 1985. *Callea*

3

The Modern Chihuahua in the United States

ALTHOUGH 21,398 CHIHUAHUAS were individually registered with the AKC in 1987, very few were exhibited. Most Chihuahuas are owned as pets and companions. Of those that were shown in 1987, 265 (includes both varieties) became Champions. In Obedience Trials, fourteen earned the Companion Dog title, three completed a Companion Dog Excellent, three garnered the Utility Dog title and one completed the requirements for a Tracking Dog title.

For many years the Chihuahua was in the top ten of the most popular breeds. After a considerable decline in registrations during the 1970s, the breed is slowly rising in popularity once again, and generally ranks between seventeenth and twentieth of all AKC breeds.

There are literally hundreds of outstanding breeders in the United States as well as in other parts of the world. In this chapter, I shall concentrate only on those in the United States, outstanding dogs from various breeders throughout the country, as well as the many dogs that have won all-breed Bests in Show and Bests of Breed at specialties. This should by no means limit one's choice of a breeder from whom to select a puppy or grown stock, to begin a breeding

An informal photo of Ch. Jacinto of Evergreen Grove, a top-winning Smooth Coat in 1987 and 1988. Breeder and now owner is Elizabeth Johnson. At the time this Smooth was being campaigned, she was co-owned by Mary Silkworth. *Terry*

Ch. MiVida's The Star Warrior, a top winner of the 1980s. Owners, Howard and Mary S. Gill. At four-and-one-half years of age, she still liked to show. *Terry*

Ch. Chaperro's El Tigre of Karma was a top-winning Long Coat of 1988, handled by Mike Walsh for owners Mary H. McGill and Karen A. Abe. Breeders are Pat and Jerry Branson. *Missy*

Ch. Chaperro's Teddy Bear-L, the Number 1 Long Coat for 1987 under the Rutledge System. Shown by Erv Dodge for owners/breeders Pat and Jerry Branson. Since Mr. Dodge's retirement, Teddy has been shown by Joe Waterman. *Bill Francis*

Ch. Bayard Alvin of Reginald RJR, Best of Winners, CCA Chicago, 1979.
Breeder/owner, Melanie Newell. Robert Caviness judged. *Ritter*

Ch. RJR Reginald of Bayard, owned by Melanie Newell, won Best of Variety at
three Specialty shows, Best Stud Dog at CCA, 1979, 1980, 1981, and several Group
placings. He sired more than twenty-seven champions. Breeder, RJR Kennels.
Noel E. Johnson

Ch. Jonhenri's Play Gypsy Play completed his title with a Group First. Shown by Sheila Peters, co-owned with M. Weisman. Breeders, G. Johnson and M. Riley.
Callea

Ch. Quantico's Black Jewel, owned by Ruth Kayser. Breeder, Mrs. C. G. "Betty" Peterson, Canada. *Ashbey*

program or advance with a particular line. Rather, the breeders mentioned herein come under one of two categories: they have demonstrated significant contributions to the breed through consistent and outstanding accomplishments in breeding and/or they have recorded achievements in the show ring. Some have gone on to even greater heights by continuing with their breed champions in obedience competition. These breeder/exhibitors cover more than three or four decades of achievement throughout the United States. Even though some of the Chihuahuas and breeders are no longer with us, they will remain in memory, accomplishments, and the canine genes that are carried on by the newer people in the breed.

BEST IN SHOW, BEST IN SPECIALTY SHOW

Although Chihuahuas had been admitted to the regular show classes at AKC events for quite some time, it was not until 1951 that the first Chihuahua won Best in Show at an all-breed event. This was a Smooth Coat Chihuahua, Ch. Attas' Gretchen, bred and owned by Mrs. Mike Attas. It took even longer for the first Long Coat Chihuahua to achieve this coveted award, when in 1975 Ch. Snow Bunny d'Casa de Cris, bred, owned and handled by Martha Hooks, won Best in Show. From 1951 to date there have been 32 Smooth Coat and four Long Coat Chihuahuas to achieve the highest all-breed award. These are listed below.

All-Breed Bests in Show

Smooth Coat Chihuahuas

> Ch. Attas' Gretchen
> Ch. La Oro Cajara De Oro
> Ch. Miss Rose Bud
> Ch. LaMay's Dagmar
> Ch. Galvern's Mona
> Ch. Shadwick's Romona
> Ch. Child's Chico Negro
> Ch. Tejano Texas Kid
> Ch. McCasland's Melodia
> Ch. Buck's Jetta

Ch. Holiday Gold Jubilee started his career at six months of age and completed his title undefeated with breeder Mary Myers. He is now owned by Sheila and Marc Weisman.   *Fox & Cook*

Ch. Holiday Gold Jubilee broke the all-time Best in Show record set in 1956. "Doc's" sixteenth Best in Show win was from judge H. Anthony Hodges with handler Joe Waterman for owners Sheila and Marc Weisman.

Rinehart

Ch. Bliss Hoosier Boy Named Sue won his first major from breeder/judge Timothy Catterson, handled by his breeder/owner, Elizabeth Bliss. Now one of only four Long Coats to win an all-breed Best in Show, he is the son of Ch. Ouachitah Beau Chiene.
Alberson

Ch. Ouachitah Beau Chiene, multiple Best in Show winner, was shown by breeder/handler Linda George for owner Nancy Shapland.
Graham

An informal photo of Ch. Ouachitah For Your Eyes Only, the first Chihuahua to win the Toy Group at Westminster, Feb. 13–14, 1984. He is pictured with his breeder/owner, Linda George.

Multiple Best in Show and multiple Specialty winner Ch. Jo-El's Drummer Boy. Handler, Terri Lyddon. Breeder/owners, Joan and Russ Kruetzman. *Petrulis*

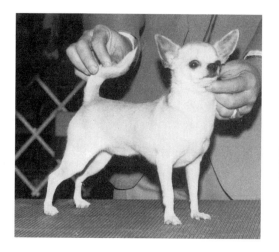

Ch. Holiday's Tijuana La Cune won Best in Show with handler James Lehman, for breeder Mary Myers. Maxwell Riddle was the judge.
Sosa

Ch. Twinkle Snowshoes Feathers; owner, Ruth Morrow. This Long Coat came from the Veterans Class at eight and one-half years old, for a CCA Best of Variety win from judge Francis Smith. *Ritter*

Ch. Dugger's Disco Dancer, Best of Winners at the CC of Atlanta, April 1979. This top quality Smooth Coat was handled by his breeder/owner, Celia Dugger. Noted breeder of long standing Carolyn Stober Hamilton judged.

Ch. Kottke's Little Sweetie Pie
Ch. Gene's Carla
Ch. Thurmer's Little Gayla
Ch. Kitty's Miss Brag A Bout
Ch. Hurd's Honey Bee
Ch. Jay's Speedy Gonzalles
Skaggs Pistol Pete
Ch. Quantico's Little Crusader
Ch. Gindon Bo-Jengles of Dartan
Ch. Quantico's Daisy Mae
Ch. Stober's Jenny of Wildwood
Ch. Dartan's Dominique D'Quachitah
Ch. Call's Delightful Design
Ch. Holiday's Tijuana La Cune
Ch. Elh's Mighty Lunar of Dartan
Ch. Ouachitah Fire and Ice
Ch. Athame's The High Priestiss
Ch. Ouachitah For Your Eyes Only
Ch. Jo-El's Drummer Boy
Ch. Jacinta of Evergreen Grove
Ch. Holiday Gold Jubilee
Ch. Dartan Strut Your Stuff

Long Coat Chihuahuas

Ch. Snow Bunny d'Casa de Cris
Ch. Flint's Little Lucky Robin
Ch. Ouachitah Beau Chiene
Ch. Bliss Hoosier Boy Named Sue

Best of Breed Winners—Chihuahua Club of America Specialty Show

Although the first Chihuahua Club of America Specialty Show was held in 1928, the records for Best of Breed at the events held between 1928 and 1934 are unavailable from the AKC. Additionally, in some years, more than one event was held.

1935   Ch. Si Si Oro Principe
1936   Ch. Alegria Pina
       Ch. Si Si Oro Principe

Ch. Hurd's Marty was handled by Marie Hurd at the 1981 spring Specialty show of the CCA. Judge Carolyn Stober Hamilton awarded him Best
of Opposite Sex to Best of Variety.

Ch. Kimball's Playboy of Dugger was shown
by owner Trudy Kimball, at the spring Specialty
show of the CCA. Judge Carolyn Stober
Hamilton awarded him Best of Opposite Sex,
in Smooth Coats.

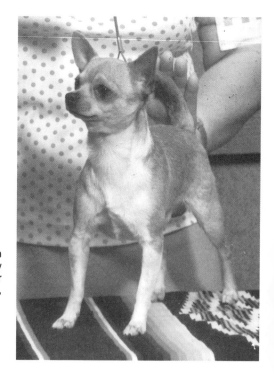

A beautiful head study of Ch. Regalaire's El Poco Marvel. Breeder/owners, Joseph Smith and Mozelle Smith.

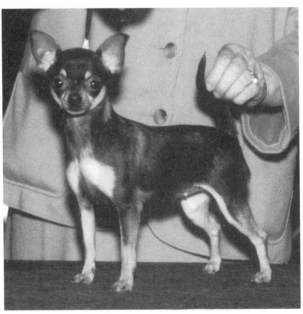

Ch. Terrymont Marsubri Ragtime won Winners at the AKC Centennial Show, in 1984. Breeders/owners, Terrymont Kennels and Marcia Greenburg. *Ashbey*

Ch. Kay's Don Feleciano-L was handled by Mike Walsh for owner Katheryne C. Darrah. Donny was a multiple Group and Specialty show winner. He is in retirement with co-owners Ruth Morrow and S. M. "Dick" Dickerson. *Rich Bergman*

Ch. Adams Joy Sundance Kid, multiple Group winner. Handled by Terence Childs for owners Rey and Viola Burgos. Breeder, Ann Freeman. *Tatham*

1937 Don Juan Patro
1938 Ch. Phoenix Chico
     Ch. Little Meron V
1939 Don Juan Alfonso
     Ch. La Rey
1940 Pate's Tu La Rosa
     Meronette
1941 Ch. El Gusto Wakita
     Ch. Meronette Grudier
1943 Ch. Oro Marinero
1944 Don Quixote Grudier
1946 Ch. Meronette Grudier
1947 Ch. La Oro Damisela
1948 Ch. La Oro Damisela
1949 Ch. Carsello's La-Zorita
1950 Thurmer's Neta
1951 Ch. Thurmer's Staar Rusty
1952 Ch. Galvern Mona
1953 Ch. Ross's Bonita Bambino
1954 Ch. Tejano Texas Kid
1955 Ch. Tejano Texas Kid
1956 Ch. Bill's Black Bart
1957 Ch. Rowe's Wee Margo De Oro
1958 Ch. Lanewood's Mister Bill
1959 Ch. Teeny Wee's Kitten
1960 Bill's Cotton Candy
1961 Ch. Belden's Tammy La Grando
1962 Ch. Eden's Timmy Lou
1963 Ch. Pardue's Master Don
1964 Ch. Langlais Goodie Goodie
1965 Ch. Averill's Bo-Bo
1966 Ch. Misalou's Little Rickey
1967 Albet's Sams-Son
1968 Beachy's Huerfanita
1969 Ch. Shroyer's Rock Robin
1970 Ch. Jay's Speedy Gonzalles
1971 Ch. Varga's Tijuana Brass
1972 Ch. Misalou's Little Amy
1973 Ch. Ervin's Frosty Snowman
1974 Ch. Gindon Bo-Jengles of Dartan
1975 Ch. Shroyer's Apache Rain Prince

Ch. Miclanjo Kaleidoscope completed her championship under judge Dr. Leon Seligman. At age six months and two days she was Best of Winners and Best of Opposite Sex to Best of Breed at the CC of Mid-Jersey, February 1985, E. Ruth Terry, judge. Shown by breeder/owner Carolyn Mooney. *Alverson*

Ch. Pittore's Harvest Dancer, Best of Breed, CCA, May 1985. Handled by Joyce McComiskey for owner/breeder Patricia Pittore. The judge was Maxine Beam. *Brodbeck*

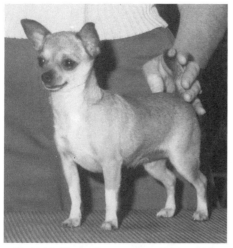

Ch. Hale's Clementine, a multiple Group winner, was shown by breeder/owner Myrle Hale. *Graham*

Ch. Dartan's Constant Comment, with Linda George handling for breeder/owners Darwin and Tanya Delaney, won the 1986 CCA Best of Breed under Beverly Lehnig. *Noel*

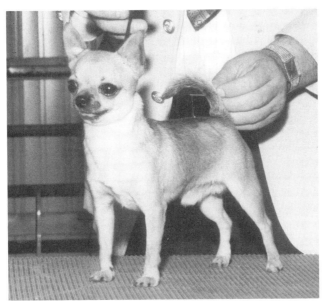

Ch. Dartan Strut Your Stuff, shown here as a top quality, very young male Smooth Coat. Breeder/owners, Darwin and Tanya Delaney. This dog later became an all-breed Best in Show winner. *Booth*

1976   Ch. Bo-Jengles Charisma of Dartan
1977   Durbin's Jack the Giant Killer
       Ch. Mea Hale's A Bonanza
1978   Ch. Caviness' Oh So Schnitzy
       Ch. Round Table The One and Only
1979   Ch. Cobtown Begonia
       Ch. Sykes' Rick Rock Rain Shroyer
1980   Ch. Dugger's Disco Dancer
       Ch. Hurd-Cobtown Red Hot Poker
1981   Ch. Call's Delightful Design
       Ch. Holiday's Tijuana La Cune
1982   Alange Asi Si Balla M-Hija
       Ch. GinJim's Royal Acres Mervyn
1983   Ch. Ouachita For Your Eyes Only (won both shows
       in 1983)
1984   Stober's Melvina of Wildwood
       Ch. Dartan's Pirate Blackbeard
1985   Ch. Pittore's Harvest Dancer
       Ch. Jo-El's Drummer Boy
1986   Ch. Miclanjo Wilhewag of Lazy VK
       Ch. Dartan's Constant Comment
1987   Stober's Truffels of Wildwood
       Ch. Kay's Don Feleciano-L
1988   Ch. Jo-El's Drummer Boy (won both shows in 1988)

4

Showing the Chihuahua in Other Countries— Their Standards and Systems

WE WILL FIRST examine the main points of the Chihuahua Standard in three countries, with a look at how the AKC Standard may differ.

THE STANDARDS

There are very few differences between the *Canadian Kennel Club Standard* and the American Kennel Club Standard. One area of difference is in the minimum size. In Canada, one pound is minimum, and if two dogs are equally good in type, the more diminutive is preferred. There is no minimum in the AKC Standard, and no size preference.

Canada: Teeth level. AKC: Teeth level or scissors bite.
Canada: Natural bobtail or tailless permissible, if so born, and not against a good dog. AKC: Natural bobtail or tailless disqualifying faults.

Can./Am./Mex. Ch. Quantico's Little Crusader, a multiple Group and Best in Show winner. Breeder Mrs. C. G. "Betty" Peterson co-owned Crusader with Carol Humphreys. *Watercolor by E. R. Terry*

40

Can./Am. Ch. Hilaire's Cher-Chayon, Canada's Number 1 Smooth Coat for 1978, also won a Specialty show in the United States. Breeder/owner, Edna St. Hilaire, Canada.
Russ Hellard

Can./Am. Ch. Hilaire's Cher-Soleil, Canada's Number 1 Smooth Coat for 1979. As a brace with his sister, Can./Am. Ch. Hilaire's Cherie-Scelle, they hold a record for most Best Brace in Show wins in the breed. *Russ Hellard*

Can./Am. Ch. Hilaire's Cherie-Cielle, Canada's Number 1 Smooth Coat in 1976, was also a winner at a U.S. Specialty. Breeder/owner, Edna St. Hilaire, Canada.

41

Can./Am. Ch. So Big of Beau Mist won Best of Variety at the CCA Specialty, October 1974, under judge Alberta "Pat" Booth. Breeder, Mrs. C. G. "Betty" Peterson. Now owned by Mrs. T. Carpenter and Alan Chambers, who was handling. *Robert Holiday*

Ch. Dear Miss Chumbley, Number 1 Long Coat in Canada for 1986, and Number 3 Long Coat for 1987. Breeder/owned by Shirley Dear, Canada. *Russ Hellard*

Canada: No mention of what to do with dogs over six pounds. AKC: Dogs over six pounds are disqualified.

The Canadian Scale of Points and the AKC Scale of Points differ considerably.

Canada has at least two specialty clubs for the breed: the Chihuahua Club of British Columbia and the Chihuahua Club of Canada. In addition, there are some clubs devoted only to Toy breeds, such as the Toy Club of Ontario and the Mount Royal Toy Dog Fanciers in the Montreal area.

In Mexico, the breed is called Chihuahueño. There is a Chihuahua club, called Chihuahueños de Mexico Asociación Civil, that is approved by the Federación Canofila Mexicana, A.C., which is the Mexican Kennel Club.

Mexico is a member of the FCI or Federation Cynologique Internationale, so uses the same Standard. *The FCI Standard* is excellent. It is detailed, well written and informative. These are some excerpts from the Standard, which was approved by the General Assembly of June 11 and 12, 1985.

Under *General Appearance:* ". . . its diminutive size, however, does not excuse any deformity, deficiency, or lack of the harmony in any of the parts. This little dog is appreciated as companion and guardian (alarm)."

There is mention of a high-strung temperament. Also Smooth Coats and Long Coats can be interbred, but are judged separately. The head is of utmost importance and very large, and the stop is very pronounced, deep and wide. "It is desirable that the lines of the muzzle, seen from the front and above, vaguely suggest angular planes." The nose is level with the stop. Any color nose is permissible. The teeth may be slightly irregular: "the absence of a few pieces due to age are tolerated if the jaws are in proper position, should not be used against a good dog." The lowest point of the ear, the center of the eye and the base of the stop are on one plane. Having ears rather low set, "muzzle sloping down in relation to the forehead (non-level)," is a fault.

"Abdomen moderately tucked up to avoid appearance of obesity. . . . The distance from brisket to withers is the same as to ground."

Gait: "Seen from behind, the hindquarters must remain in almost parallel planes, increasing the angle of incidence according to the increase of the speed. . . . Coming and going, the legs must not

Can./Am. Ch. Hilaire's Cher-Pistache sired many champions and was a consistent Group placer. Breeder/owner, Edna St. Hilaire. *Russ Hellard*

Can./Am. Ch. Hilaire's Cherie-Scelle, Canada's Number 1 Smooth Coat for 1982 and 1983; Number 1 Toy Dog for 1983. She is a multiple Best in Show winner. Breeder/owner, Edna St. Hilaire, Canada.

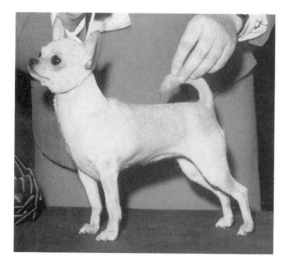

Can./Am. Ch. Hilaire's Celeste of Edge began her career at six months with a Group First and Best Puppy in Show. She was undefeated and Number 1 Smooth Coat in Canada in 1987. In 1988 she won Toy Groups and Best in Show. She was Best of Breed at the first Specialty show of the Chihuahua Club of British Columbia in 1988. She was handled by Mary B. White for Edna St. Hilaire. *Lindt*

Ch. Yetagen Yarry was the top Smooth Coat and the top Smooth Coat Stud Dog in 1987, owned by Vera Gillott and Melton Mowbray, United Kingdom. Yarry has won twenty-five CCs as of this writing.

Ch. Yetagen Yogan, a Finnish and Danish Champion owned by Vera Gillott, United Kingdom. Yogan was the first Smooth Coat ever to win Best in Show all-breeds in Finland.

Ch. Yeosinga Tomahawk. This young red-and-white dog was the top Long Coat puppy "Our Dogs" 1987. He won his crowning Challenge Certificate at the South Wales All-Breeds Championship Show, July 1988. Owners, Brian Leonard and Francis Yeoh, United Kingdom. *Teoh*

Ch. Yeosinga Spellbinder. This gold sable dog was the top Long Coat in 1987. Owners, Messrs. Brian W. Leonard and Francis Yeoh, United Kingdom. Spellbinder was Best in Show at the UK Toy show, 1987. *Teoh*

move too close to each other, interfering with the normal flow of the movement. . . ." Hackney trot must be penalized.

Major faults listed under legs: cow hocks, patella luxation, dysplasia.

Tail: "The shape, characteristic of the breed, gives the impression of being flat, wider in the middle than at the base, tapering to a point. This flat appearance is a result of the lateral position of the hairs, longer than on the rest of the body. . . . The tail is important in all its details because it gives harmony and balance to the ensemble."

Disqualifications: Weight over three kilograms. "Ears drooping or amputated. Lack of tail, natural or artificial. Baldness. Extreme deer-type specimens." Long Coats have an added disqualification: long hair on face.

The Scale of Points is interesting because it allows 15 points for temperament in both coats.

We are unable to include the *Kennel Club* (Great Britain) *Standard* verbatim, as the Club will not permit unrestricted printing. This does not prevent comments being made about the British Standard, however. It does mention temperament in a manner similar to the AKC Standard, but adds that the breed should not snap, nor should it be shy. Nor is a level bite allowed. Only one tail carriage, over the back, is permissible. Where the AKC Standard calls for a moderately long tail and moderately long nails, the British Standard calls for a medium length tail and moderately short nails. It specifies that hackney gait or high stepping is not allowed. Although convergence of legs is not directly specified, it is mentioned that legs are neither too close, nor too wide, when gaiting, which seems to indicate some convergence toward a center line is expected. There is no minimum weight, and no disqualification for being over six pounds (although it prefers two to four pounds in weight). It also prefers the more diminutive when dogs are otherwise equal, as in the Canadian and Mexican/FCI Standards.

There are several Chihuahua specialty clubs associated with the Kennel Club in England and some of these have as many as 500 members:

The British Chihuahua Club
Chihuahua Club of Scotland
Chihuahua Club of South Wales
Midland Chihuahua Club

Can./Am. Ch. Elsdyle Oriole, top Long Coat in Canada for 1987. Breeder, Mrs. B. M. Morgan, United Kingdom; owner, M. Eileen Taylor, Canada. *McKnight*

Can./Am. Ch. Hack's Pack The Dallas Kid, owned by Shirley Dear and Anne Stober. Breeders, Tad and Peggy Hackelton. Mrs. Dear is active in the Pet Therapy Program in Canada, taking her Chihuahuas to visit nursing homes.

Ch. Holiday Clark Gable. Breeder, Mary Myers, U.S.A.; owner, H. Yanase, Japan.

A beautiful free-standing pose by Ch. Shillmaine's Pocatello, a tri-color. At the time of this photo he was owned by Maureen Samuels, Canada.

Northern Counties Chihuahua Club
Ulster Chihuahua Club
West Country Chihuahua Club
Long Coat Chihuahua Club
Smooth Coat Chihuahua Club

EXHIBITING IN OTHER COUNTRIES

All countries that are members of the FCI use the same Standard. In the most simple description, to qualify for the FCI championship, for breeds not subject to Working Trials, a dog must obtain 4 CACIBs, which, loosely translated, are champion certificates of international beauty. These must be given by three different judges in three different countries, with one of the four CACIBs "obtained in the owner's country of residence or in the country of origin of the breed. However, small countries, where few shows are held, may choose a neighboring country in which the CACIB may be obtained." This is a direct quote from the FCI rules. A period of at least one year and one day must elapse between the first and last CACIB. The rules are somewhat different for Dachshunds, Fox Terriers and Working Dogs.

It is not possible to exhibit in all the countries that are associated with the FCI because some of these countries have quarantine regulations.

To become a Canadian Champion a dog must earn 10 points under at least three different judges at three different shows. The points may be earned at either Breed or Group level. In Canada, dogs may earn points at any of the Group placements. In addition, unless excused by the Show Superintendent, the Best of Breed Chihuahua must compete in the Group or all awards and prizes are canceled.

Again, keep in mind that the aforementioned is described in the simplest of terms.

There are several types of dog shows in Great Britain: Exemption Shows; Matches; Primary Shows; Sanction Shows; Limited Shows; Open Shows; and Championship Shows. It is only at the latter that Kennel Club Challenge Certificates are awarded. There are also Field Trials and Obedience Shows. To become a breed champion in Great Britain "a dog must obtain 3 Challenge Certificates under 3 different judges with at least one of the Challenge Certificates (CCs) being awarded when the dog was over 12 months

RAAD VAN BEHEER
OP KYNOLOGISCH GEBIED IN NEDERLAND
Postbus 5901 · 1007 AX Amsterdam Z.
Postgiro 71442 · Telefoon 644471

STAMBOOM van de CHIHUAHUA (KORTHAAR)

JWS
1-1 NAAM: "RIO DESIERTO DEL PERRO"

N.H.S.B. 1:5 3 2.0 8 8
(Nederlands Hondenstamboek)

VADER

1 Ned.en Int.Kamp.
El la Qwinta's
Little Tommy W'83
N.H.S.B. 1.156.784

3 Yaverland Master
Mariner of Oaxaca
KCSB 161 BQ

4 Rumawill Plaza
Imp.(Eng.)1.149.767
KCR D 290651 D 7

7 Yaverland Smokiblue
KCR 77870/74

8 Yaverland Gingerella
KCR 155039/75

9 Rumawill Peter Piper
KCSB 2246 BM

10 Taradona Prudence
KCR B 172781 C 10

MOEDER

2 Noble's
Chocolate Chip

N.H.S.B. Imp.(Am.)
1.460.027
AKC TC 464163

5 Thome's Sweet Pea
AKC TC 116269

6 Thome's Chiquita
AKC TB 791594

11 Hutchens Sugar Daddy-I
AKC TB 374030
Am.Kamp.

12 Thome's Gordito
AKC TB 791595

13 Ledfords Carlos
AKC TB 467635

14 Ledfords Ci Ji Kay
AKC TB 206626

Nest no. : 4480
Geslacht : reu.
Tat. no. : e LO 1125.
Kleur : wit.
Geboren : 25 mei 1987 (1900 zeven en tachtig)
Fokker : M.Leest-Noble,
Marijkestraat 11,
Moerdijk
Eigenaar : Fokker.

Amsterdam, 14 september 1987

De Secretaris
van de Raad van Beheer

Opgelet z.o.z.

A Dutch pedigree from Margery Leest, The Netherlands, issued by the Raad Van Beheer Op Kynologisch Gebied in Nederland.

51

of age. The judge will decide which dog wins the Challenge Certificate for its sex and it should be appreciated that a Challenge Certificate is not a class award but a separate competition. The judge will decide which of the dogs entered in the breed classification are to be considered for the Challenge Certificate award." Dogs must be registered with the Kennel Club before they can be shown at a Kennel Club–licensed show other than an Exemption Show. There are many more breed classes in the United Kingdom than in the United States. All champions are shown in the Open Class with nonchampions.

In Holland, the Kennel Club is called Raad Van Beheer Op Kynologisch Gebied in Nederland. The Dutch shorten it to Raad Van Beheer. It is a member of the FCI. To become a Dutch champion, the Chihuahua must win four CACs, which are National Championship Certificates, in various combinations of types of shows. Not all shows award the CAC. The last CAC must be won after the dog has reached the age of twenty-seven months.

There are two types of kennel clubs in Holland: breed specialty clubs (only one allowed per breed) and all-breed clubs. The country is divided into regions with one all-breed club per region.

The Winner Show is held once a year and is sponsored by the Raad Van Beheer. Winners Dog and Winners Bitch are awarded double certificates, and the Reserve Winner gets one certificate toward its championship.

Shows are run by the kennel clubs. When entries close, and just before the show, an exhibitor receives one card per dog, which includes the dog's number and class, as well as the name and address of the owner. These cards are presented at the show, which usually opens at 8:00 A.M., and dogs are in by 9:30 A.M. Shows may have between 1,000 and 2,500 dogs. The veterinarian checks the dogs upon arrival. Time schedules for classes are obtained at the shows, which are benched.

Classes in the National or International Shows have a minimum dog's age of nine months. The "match type" shows are unlike AKC matches, as points are awarded, and have a six-month minimum age. However, the six-to-nine-months winner cannot compete for Best in Show.

Classes at the shows are: nine to eighteen months; Open (fifteen months plus); Breeder's Class (nine months minimum); Champion Class (fifteen months and over, with at least one championship title); Utility Class (for some breeds). In Holland, championship certificates may be collected from nine months of age, but for the international title, fifteen months is the minimum.

Dutch, German, Belgian, International Champion in Europe, Diente de Plata el Limbo. Breeder/owner, Mrs. M. H. R. Silverentand, The Netherlands. *L. J. J. Smeets*

Dutch, Belgian, International Champion, Heddachi's Happy Highwayman. Dutch top Smooth Coat, 1987. Won the Winner shows, Amsterdam, 1987, and Brussels, 1987. Breeder, H. O. Schevenhoven. Owner, Margery Leest, The Netherlands.

Can./Am. Ch. Shillmaine's Tuscarora, bred and owned by Maureen Samuels and shown by Capt. A. M. W. Samuels. He completed his American championship with three majors.

Can./Am. Ch. Shillmaine's Sacajaweo, Canadian Group winner, owned by Mrs. M. T. Samuels, bred by Capt. A. M. W. Samuels, Canada.

The F.C.I. International Championship Certificate.

The judge dictates a report on each dog. One copy is given to the exhibitor and the other to the kennel club. There are four qualifications: excellent, very good, good and those that just make the Standard. The steward writes the placing and qualifications on a blackboard.

Best of Breed goes into the Ring of Honor, which is comparable to the AKC Group. Braces are called Couples and are composed of one male and one female. Three or more dogs are designated as a Group. These may be of any sex. There are Junior Handling Classes, and some club match shows have a Children's Costume Parade, in which the participants wear costumes of the breed's country of origin.

Dutch dogs must be tattooed to be registered with the Raad Van Beheer. The letters go in one ear and numbers are placed in the other ear.

Following is a simplified comparison of comparable requirements for championships in various countries:

FCI (International): 4 CACIBs from 3 countries; at least one from own country or country of origin of the breed; 3 different judges, 1 year between first and last CACIB, minimum age 15 months.

Holland: 4 CACs, minimum age 9 months, the last one after 27 months, 2 different judges.

Belgium: 3 CACIBs, 1 year between first and last certificates, 2 different judges, 1 win must occur in Brussels.

Monaco: 2 certificates, but there is only one show per year.

Austria: 3 certificates, 1 year between first and last, 2 different judges.

France: 4 certificates, 1 awarded in a designated city, 3 different judges.

Spain: 3 certificates with 1 earned in Madrid, 2 different judges, no time limit.

Portugal: 3 certificates, 2 different judges, no time limit.

The World Title is awarded only at the yearly World Show, which is held in a different country each year.

5

The Chihuahua Standard in the United States

THE STANDARD for any breed tells us a great many things about that particular breed. It is our past, our present, and our future. The Standard tells us where our dogs came from and their purpose; where our breed is today and where it is going. A Standard should not be taken lightly. Past breeders and founders of a single breed club spent a great deal of time trying to present an ideal picture of the breed as it emerged from obscurity to recognition by the Chihuahua Club of America and the American Kennel Club. These dedicated fanciers and breeders tried to present a clear and concise word picture and guide for future breeders to follow and for dog show judges to interpret.

It is not possible to provide a completely in-depth description in the actual Standard, for it is the workings of many people who must agree on how a breed should appear to others. Anyone who has ever served on a committee of any kind knows that it is impossible for the entire committee to agree on all the parts of a project. There must be some compromise among the various breeders when they write and try to interpret the wording of a breed Standard for others. Sometimes what seems like an insignificant part at the time is left out.

This may become an important feature at a later date. When this occurs, it is time to have a Standard revision, or a clarification of some sort. Hence, breed Standards for today's dog may not represent the dog of yesteryear.

It is important that Standards not be changed willy-nilly for the whims of a few. It is only when an important part of the dog has undergone a significant change, so that it no longer bears resemblance to the current written words, that there should be any revisions made. Finally, those changes must be agreed upon by a large majority of members of the Parent Club.

Standards should be written that last a long time. If our dogs' traits, characteristics and type are changing frequently, then breeders are not adhering to the Standard in their breeding programs.

The Standard of each breed must define its type and character as accurately as possible. By this definition breeders should plan their breeding programs and judges should evaluate the dogs. The correct type will include a description of size, color, structure, gait, temperament, soundness, balance and any characteristics unique for the breed.

My preference for a breed Standard is to have it laid out in the somewhat general order in which the dog is judged, as that makes it much easier to evaluate each specimen quickly. For example, purpose of the breed; general appearance, including characteristics, temperament and size; head, including the sum parts as eyes, ears, skull, muzzle, bite, expression, neck; forequarters and feet; body, including topline and backline; hindquarters, including feet (in some breeds the hind feet are drastically different from the front feet); tail; coat; color; gait/movement; faults; disqualifications or penalties. A personal note here is that my preference is for no disqualifications. The decision should be left to the judge to determine if the particular specimen is within the Standard for the breed.

In this author's opinion, in our current Standard as of 1989 there are serious omissions, such as failure to indicate the presence of a stop. There are descriptions that no longer pertain to our breed, as they have been bred out over the years or breeders no longer consider certain descriptions as essential in describing the Chihuahua as it exists today. For example, at one time there was a passage that read, "one to six pounds, with two to four pounds preferred." Today's American breeders feel that as long as the breed stays six pounds and under there should be no minimum, only a maximum. They reason perhaps that bitches closer to six pounds are needed to perpetuate the breed by easy whelpings and that these larger sizes should not be penalized. The author has found, however, that one cannot determine by the size of the bitch whether or not she is capable of reproducing easily. The size of the pelvis, position of puppy, plus dilation of the bitch during whelping are of more use in determining whelping ease. Therefore, a small bitch should not be penalized for size when being judged.

At the same time, males should not be penalized for size either, as long as they stay within the six-pound limit. A very tiny male may or may not be capable of continuous stud service, but if he is within the six-pound Standard limit, then he should be judged accordingly. A larger male, if of superior quality, should not be put down to a tiny male of inferior quality.

In the show ring, the size of the Chihuahua should not matter at all, as long as it is within the six-pound limit. It is possible for a small bitch to whelp normally; or it may be that a large bitch will need a Caesarian section due to medical complications, or poor structure beyond her size. Dog show judges have no way to make these determinations, so their judgments should be made strictly on the type, characteristics and the soundness of the Chihuahua and not on its size. In fact, some breeders feel it is difficult to obtain physical soundness in the very tiny specimens.

The Standard was revised in 1972 by the Chihuahua Club of America and approved by the American Kennel Club.

The Chihuahua Club of America, Inc., Official Breed Standard

Head: A well-rounded "apple dome" skull, with or without molera. Cheeks and jaws lean. Nose moderately short, slightly pointed (self-colored in blond types, or black). In moles, blues, and chocolates, they are self-colored. In blond types, pink nose permissible.

Ears: Large, held erect when alert, but flaring at the sides at about an angle of 45 degrees when in repose. This gives breadth between the ears. In *Long Coats,* ears fringed. (Heavily fringed ears may be tipped slightly, never down.)

Eyes: Full, but not protruding, balanced, set well apart—dark ruby, or luminous. (Light eyes in blond types permissible.)

Teeth: Level or scissors bite. Overshot or undershot bite or any distortion of the bite should be penalized as a serious fault.

Neck and Shoulders: Slightly arched, gracefully sloping into lean shoulders, may be smooth in the very short types, or with ruff about neck preferred. In *Long Coats,* large ruff on neck desired and preferred. Shoulders lean, sloping into a slightly broadening support above straight forelegs that are set well under, giving a free play at the elbows. Shoulders should be well up, giving balance and soundness, sloping into a level back. (Never down or low.) This gives a chestiness, and strength of forequarters, yet not of the "Bulldog" chest; plenty of brisket.

Back and Body: Level back, slightly longer than height. Shorter backs desired in males. Ribs rounded (but not too much "barrel-shaped").

Hindquarters: Muscular, with hocks well apart, neither out nor in, well let down, with firm sturdy action.

Tail: Moderately long, carried sickle either up or out, or in a loop over the back, with tip just touching the back. (Never tucked under.) Hair on tail in harmony with the coat of the body, preferred furry in *Smooth Coats.* In *Long Coats,* tail full and long (as a plume).

Feet: Small, with toes well split up but not spread, pads cushioned, with fine pasterns. (Neither the hare nor the cat-foot.) A dainty, small foot with nails moderately long.

Coat: In the *Smooth,* the coat should be soft texture, close and glossy. (Heavier coats with undercoats permissible.) Coat placed well over body with ruff on neck, and more scanty on head and ears. In *Long Coats,* the coat should be of a soft texture, either flat or slightly curly, with undercoat preferred. Ears fringed (heavily fringed ears may be tipped slightly, never down), feathering on feet and legs, and pants on hind legs. Large ruff on neck desired and preferred. Tail full and long (as a plume).

Color: Any color—solid, marked or splashed.

Weight: A well-balanced little dog not to exceed 6 pounds.

General Appearance: A graceful, alert, swift-moving little dog with saucy expression. Compact, and with terrierlike qualities.

Scale of Points

Head, including ears	20
Body, including tail	20
Coat	20
Legs	20
General Appearance and Action	20
TOTAL	100

Disqualifications

Cropped tail, bobtail.
Broken down or cropped ears.
Any dog over 6 pounds in weight.
In *Long Coats*, too thin coat that resembles bareness.

Approved November 14, 1972

6

Interpretation of the Chihuahua Standard— Critique and Comparison

THE FOLLOWING is an interpretation of the Chihuahua Standard as it is presently set forth and approved by the Chihuahua Club of America and the American Kennel Club, according to the last revision of 1972.

Our standard tells us that if we take a Long Coat Chihuahua and cut the coat down, we will have a Smooth Coat Chihuahua. According to the AKC Standard, it should be the same dog, with or without the extra coat. The difference between the two varieties lies in the length of coat, including fringe and feathering, and, in Long Coats only, too thin coat that resembles bareness. Also, in Long Coats only, heavily fringed ears may be tipped. Basically, the two varieties should appear to be the same.

No perfect dog has ever been produced, so while we have a Standard of Excellence that gives us the ideal, or perfect dog, we must still deal with the real world. When judges step into the ring to officiate, they will be faced with a wide range of type. How wide a parameter to accept will be open for discussion, but here we will

Ch. Tejano Texas Kid, shown in the mid-fifties, held the record
for the most Best in Show awards for over thirty years. Handled by Clara Alford for owners Mr. and Mrs. Bob Roberts.

Terry

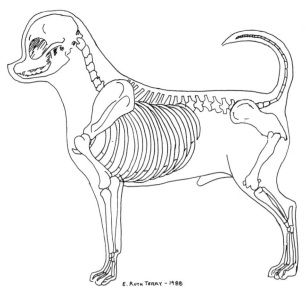

Skeleton of the Chihuahua.   *Terry*

There should be the conformation of a Smooth Coat underneath the coat of a Long Coat Chihuahua.   *Terry*

attempt to portray just how wide a range is acceptable. The author believes in a slight range of acceptability, relative to the ideal, for each part of the dog. Place these parameters in perspective and put them together for a whole dog that comes within a satisfactory but slight variation in quality of type, character, balance and soundness. The range of acceptability must not be extreme, but rather deviate just slightly from the ideal.

Head: Although the Standard says well-rounded, this is not a perfectly round head, but rather more like an apple shape, with or without the molera, an opening in the top of the skull. Usually, the more extreme the head, the larger the molera present. Flatter-skulled dogs are not typical.

In very young puppies, the head will appear to be a little too large for the body, as in human babies, but as the puppy matures, the body will "grow into" the head to make a well-balanced animal. Cheeks and jaws are lean, with clean lines; they are not flat.

Eyes: There is enough bony structure around the deep eye sockets so that the eyes can be large and round without protruding. They are set wide apart. They may be of any color in accordance with the color of the dog. Usually, they are luminous dark or luminous ruby, meaning, when referring to luminous, shining, bright and reflective. However, many times on chocolates, you may see an eye with a slight greenish cast, even lemon-like. Although this should not be objectionable, it is usually a matter of personal preference. The center of the eyes should be in line with the stop and the lowest part of the ear.

Ears: Our Standard says that the ears are at 45 degrees when at *rest.* This differs from the Papillon Standard, which states that the ears are at 45 degrees when *alert.*

The ear part of the Chihuahua is one of the areas that is least understood. Because the description in the American Standard refers both to the *ear set* and the *ear carriage* without specifically using those two words, it confuses those who read and interpret the Standard. The *set* is the junction of the skull and the ear lobe. The *carriage* is how the ears are held, or carried.

Chihuahua ears are set low, but generally are carried high, particularly in the show ring, where the dog is usually very alert. Thus, many people think the Chihuahua ears are high-set.

The low-set, flaring ears come off the side of the head at a 45-degree angle when the ears are in the *resting* position. The most common description of the angle is that the ears in the resting 45-degree position will approximately aim toward the ten o'clock

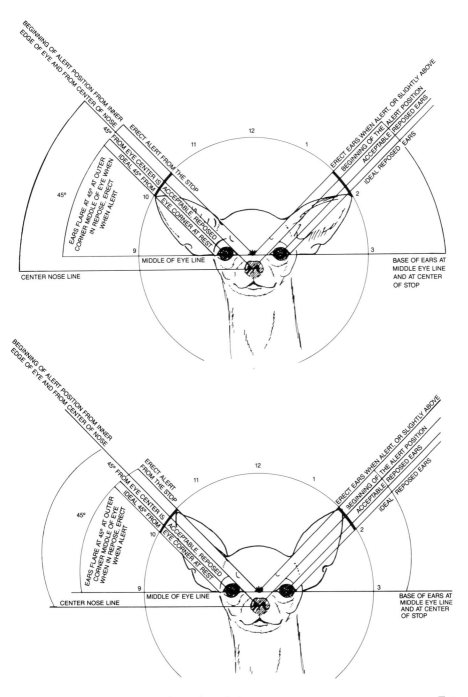

Chihuahua ear set at rest; ear carriage when alert.   *Terry*

65

and two o'clock position on a clock face. But this can be misleading, because it depends from where the angle is taken and where the dog's head was located on the clock. It is possible to place the head on the clock face somewhat differently, and still end up with a 45-degree flare at the side. Thus we have different theories regarding positions, measurements and angles, although the results may be similar.

The 45-degree flare can be easily seen if the mid-center line of the eyes is directly drawn through the stop to nine o'clock and three o'clock, and the angle is taken from the outer corner of the eye. An acceptable relaxed (repose) position could also approximate a slight rise above ten o'clock and two o'clock. The ears in the alert mode will begin to rise toward eleven and one o'clock.

When the Chihuahua's ears are in the *very* alert mode, they may come up to eleven and one o'clock. Do not confuse this alert position with a high ear set. Ears that aim close to noon, however, are usually set too high. Ears aiming to nine and three o'clock are most likely set too low. Ears may taper to either slightly rounded or slightly pointed tips.

When gaiting, or if the dog is tense, it is not unusual for the ears to flatten out against the skull. Dogs should not be penalized for this, as it is a natural occurrence.

In Smooth Coats, if the body coat is single, the ears, sides of forehead, chest, and stomach may have little or no hair. This is not considered too sparse a coat in Smooths when there is no undercoat. Bare spots in those areas in a Long Coat would be considered a very serious fault, and depending on the degree of baldness, may come under the disqualifying fault section of the Standard: "too thin a coat that resembles bareness." The color blue frequently produces coats that are not so abundant as the other colors.

In Long Coats, the ears are fringed, and may be slightly tipped, if heavily fringed; but this is a rare occurrence. This tipped ear is what one must watch out for. Be certain the ears are tipped because they are heavily fringed, not because the ears are soft. The ear leather should be strong.

The fringe on a Long Coat's ears should not loop over like an upside-down U, nor should it start very high up on the ear. That is the kind of fringe you would see on a Papillon. On a Long Coat Chihuahua there are only slight wisps of feathering near the upper part of the ear, with the main fringe begining about halfway down, and flowing out from the ear. It is not a high, lace-curtain effect, nor as full in feathering as on the Papillon.

There should be enough of an apple-domed skull to give

breadth between the ears. On the Long Coat, hair growing toward the inner ear from the sides of the forehead may give the appearance of ears being too small. A common practice is for exhibitors to trim this hair to bring out the true size of the ear. Trimming or not trimming is an exhibitor's prerogative and should not be penalized either way. The author's preference is for no ear trimming.

Muzzle: There is no mention of a stop in the present AKC Standard, but there should be a stop that is considered definite. The more extreme heads may possibly have a deeper stop, but it should not be as deep as one that is found on flat-faced breeds. In the American Standard, the muzzle is incorrectly called the nose.

The muzzle should come out from the skull at about a 90-degree angle. This would be considered ideal. But here again, we must stress parameters. A muzzle that comes within an 80-degree downward slope *might* be considered an acceptable muzzle, only if it is moderately short in relation to the head. Occasionally we might see a muzzle at a very slightly higher than 90 degree angle. This usually results in some distortion of the teeth and too strong an underjaw. A muzzle that has the nose level with the stop is best.

Once the muzzle starts getting lower than an 80-degree downward angle to the skull, however, we begin to see muzzles that become snipier, too long and too narrow. The more the muzzle points downward, the more these faults appear. What usually goes with this longer and narrower muzzle is a flatter skull and less of a stop. Usually, these dogs have much larger ears. This is more the type of Chihuahua head that was seen in the early part of the century.

Teeth: Level or scissors bite is acceptable. Overshot, undershot or any distortion of the bite should be penalized as a serious fault, according to the AKC Standard. The bite has always been a touchy subject among breeders and judges. Some feel that if no distortion shows on the outside of the jawline, a tooth out of line is not that important. It is felt that what is important is that any distortion inside the mouth, however slight, should not show on the outside. For example, distortions that cause a protruding underjaw, an excessively overlapping upper jaw, a wry jaw, too strong an underjaw or too weak an underjaw should be penalized severely.

A *scissor bite* is most common with the Chihuahua mouth. Jaws are of equal length, and the upper teeth overlap the lower teeth, with the inside surface of the upper incisors meeting the outside surface of the lower incisors. Teeth should be evenly positioned without crowding.

A *reverse scissor bite* occurs when the lower jaw is a little longer

Muzzle at right angle to head is better than that sloping downward. *Terry*

than the upper jaw, and the upper incisors are behind the lower incisors, with the outer surface of the upper incisors in direct contact with the inner surface of the lower incisors.

A *level bite* is one in which the upper and lower incisors meet edge to edge when the mouth is closed. This is the most common interpretation of a level bite.

With an *overshot bite,* the upper incisors are considerably ahead of the lower incisors, creating a space between, with no contact between upper and lower teeth. This usually results in a weak under-jaw, with a longer upper jaw.

An *undershot bite* is one in which the lower incisors protrude considerably ahead of the upper incisors. The lower jaw then becomes excessively strong, and is usually longer than the upper jaw. With an undershot bite there would be no contact between upper and lower incisors; rather, there would be a space between them.

Neck and Shoulders: The neck should be slightly arched and long enough so the head does not look as though it were sitting right on the shoulders. The medium-length neck helps to give the dog balance. A neck that is too short will make the Chihuahua look heavy in front. The neck is smooth and without folds, and the shoulder blade is rather long. The ruff on the neck should show on the Smooth Coat as well as the Long Coat, but of course to a much lesser degree. If the Smooth Coat does not have an undercoat, the ruff will be more sparse than that of a Smooth Coat with an under-coat. The Smooth Coat ruff should not be cut off.

The ruff on the Long Coat should be quite extensive, going at least to the pro-sternum and frilling out in a halo-like effect.

The lean shoulders should slope backward smoothly at enough of an angle to provide free and easy movement.

Chest: The chest is medium broad, without it being bulldoggy. The brisket should extend down to the elbow, and there should be depth to the chest. Overweight dogs will appear to be excessively heavy up front.

Back and Body: The description in the American Standard is very poor. It states level back, slightly longer than height. Shorter backs desired in males. Ribs rounded (but not too much "barrel-shaped"). By comparison, the British Standard is better in description. It states "level back. Body, from point of shoulder to rear point of croup, slightly longer than height at withers." The precise description of the measuring points in the British Standard should be adopted in the United States. The word "shorter" in the sentence "Shorter backs desired in males" does not mean "short bodies" in males. The word "back" is what causes confusion in this description. The author believes that *"somewhat shorter* bodies" is what the original writers of the Standard really meant when they wrote "shorter backs desired in males." In fact, when the dog is measured from the point of the shoulder to the point of the croup, this should be longer than the measurement from withers to ground.

By comparison to bitches, the body may seem to be only a tad longer than height, just deviating from the square. In other words, male or female, the Chihuahua should be slightly longer in body than height at the withers, measuring from point of shoulder to the rearmost point of buttocks. The height is measured from the highest point of the withers to the ground.

The backline, from withers to onset of tail, is level.

Descriptive terms are open to interpretation by breeders and judges alike. Terms such as "too long," "slightly longer," "moderately short," "somewhat wide," are all open to interpretation. You have to train your eye for visual measuring, so you will be able to recognize what is a balanced dog for the particular breed being observed.

Are legs too short or is the body too long? If you are unable to decide this point, it is more important that you recognize whether or not the dog is balanced. However, usually, if the legs are too short, there will be an excessive thickening, or dwarfism, at the wrist area. If the body is too long, then that portion of the leg will be of normal thickness. If the legs are too short, there will also be an appearance of the body having too much depth, or thickness. That is, from withers to lowest part of chest will appear to be too thick.

Forelegs: Forelegs are straight and set well under the chest. The elbows are not snug against the ribcage but rather away, so there is some free play here, while not being out at the elbows.

Hind Legs: The hind legs should have a good muscular look and feel. Dogs that are caged all the time, with little exercise, will not have these well-formed muscles. Hocks are well let down and wide apart when standing. They should not turn either in or out, but be in a straight line. There should be a sense of strength to the hindquarters. The rear is well angulated, but in keeping with the forequarters.

Feet: The feet are small, dainty, with the toes well split up. That does not mean splayed feet. The feet are neither round like a cat, nor elongated like a hare, but rather partway between the two. The pasterns are fine, yet strong and flexible, without being broken down.

Dog in correct proportion seems just right because tail
is carried sickle up. Check the measurements; they are
correct.   *Terry*

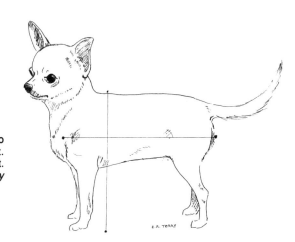

Dog in correct proportion may seem too
long in body when tail is carried sickle out.
Check the measurements; they are correct.
                                           Terry

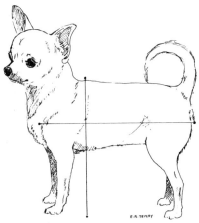

Dog in correct proportion may seem short in body when
tail is up and over, touching the back. Check the
measurements; they are correct.   *Terry*

The American Standard calls for nails moderately long. This is not an important feature, so penalty is not recommended, whether long or short nails. A Long Coat Chihuahua's feet should be feathered, although many exhibitors trim the feet for neatness, they say. The author's preference is to leave the foot feathering on. Pad hair may be trimmed to prevent splayed feet.

Tail: Americans say the tail is moderately long. The tail set is high, a little thicker in the middle before tapering to a point. At one time, this middle thickening was considered to be one of the proofs that the dog was a pure-bred Chihuahua. The Smooth Coat tail should be furry, more coated on the sides, with a flatness on the underside, a distinct characteristic of the smooth variety. The Long Coat tail should have a good plume and be in keeping with the density of the body coat. If the tail plume is not extensive, then the body coat usually is also less dense and long.

In the United States the Chihuahua is allowed three tail carriages. Do not confuse this with tail set. The acceptable carriages are: outward sickle-like; upward sickle-like, almost 90 degrees to the body; or up and curving over the back, with the tip just touching the back. In actuality, it is not important that the tip touch the back. The tail should never be tucked under between the hind legs.

Depending on the tail carriage, one dog may look too short in body (with tail over the back); another may look too long (with tail carried sickle outward); and another may look just right (tail carried sickle upward at about 90 degrees to the body). These three tail carriages become optical illusions. Eye training in the three tail carriage positions is of utmost importance to determine proportion and balance of the dog.

Coat: Coats should be soft, close and glossy. Dogs with undercoats will have a thicker, more dense coat. It should be well placed all over the dog, but in dogs that do not have an undercoat, particularly in Smooths, it may be more sparse on head, ears, tail, chest and underbelly. The Long Coats are also of soft texture, but the coat may be either flat or curly, and an undercoat is preferred. There is fringing at ears and feathering on legs and feet. The pants on hind legs should be in harmony with body coat; the ruff is large and full. The amount of feathering should be in keeping with the body coat. A coat that is too thin, resembling bareness, is a disqualification on the Long Coat variety only.

It is contradictory that under the heading of shoulders the Standard says (referring to coat), "may be smooth in the very short types, or with ruff about neck preferred . . ." and then, for tail, it says,

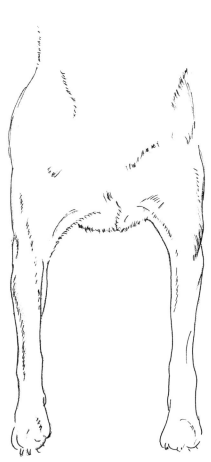

Standing position; straight front. *Terry*

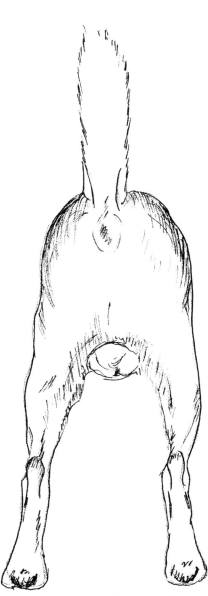

Rear standing position. Shows that it is strong
and muscular. *Terry*

"hair on tail in harmony with coat of the body, preferred furry in smooth coats." It calls for preferred neck ruff, and preferred furry tail in Smooth Coats, yet it also says smooth (referring to coat) in the very short types; tail in harmony with body coat, but preferred furry and undercoats permissible. If a ruff about neck is preferred and if a furry tail is preferred, then the dog *must* have an undercoat, or these two things could not possibly occur to any degree. These contradictory descriptions are in three different sections of the Standard and certainly must cause confusion to new breeders and new judges.

Color: Color is immaterial. Any color, solid, marked or splashed, in any configuration. All manner of markings are acceptable. If you know the specific details of the Chihuahua Standard well, you will not mistake a Chihuahua for a Papillon, no matter if the color and/or markings are similar. A judge must not fault a dog for color or markings.

Gait: Other than graceful and swift moving, there is no mention of gait in the Standard.

While moving at a trot, the backline should remain strong and level. There is good front reach when the forelegs swing straight forward, and there is strong rear drive with the rear pads showing.

The legs converging toward a center midline will be from slight to moderate convergence, according to speed. The faster the trot, the more the convergence, but they must not single-track, nor come too close together.

The Chihuahua is a double tracking dog, even when converging toward a midline under the body. Coming and going, the front and rear legs should be directly behind each other, so that only the legs nearest the judge can be seen. In other words, when coming toward you, rear legs are directly behind the front legs so only the front legs are seen. When going away, the front legs are directly behind the rear legs so only the rear legs are seen.

From the side view, feet do not come very high off the ground. On an average-size dog—i.e., four pounds—feet that go higher than roughly two inches off the ground usually result in a stiff, high goose step or in a hackney-type gait. When the feet are raised excessively high, the dog is pushed upward more than forward, thus wasting energy and covering less ground. High-stepping dogs should be penalized.

When the Chihuahua is stacked, or set up in a natural rested stance, front feet may just slightly turn outward. This will give a truer, straight movement. Feet that point exactly straight ahead

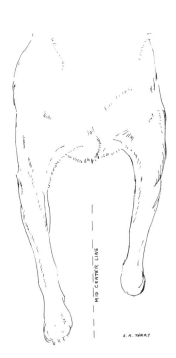

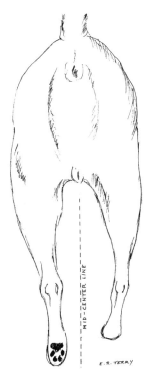

Front movement showing line of convergence. Note that the rear legs are directly behind the front legs and cannot be seen. The amount of convergence is determined by the speed of the dog. Chihuahuas double-track, even when converging. *Terry*

Moving away, with line of convergence. Note that the front legs are directly behind the rear legs and cannot be seen. Convergence is determined by the speed of the dog, but the dog still double-tracks. *Terry*

Gait. Chihuahua feet travel close to the ground; they are not high-stepping dogs. Front legs swing straight forward; rear legs have good drive.

75

while the dog is in a natural stance usually will toe inward when moving. Excessive east-west foot stance, at rest, should be penalized.

Reexamination: Chihuahuas must be examined on the table only. If the judge wants to go over the dog again, it must not be done while the dog is on the ground. Chihuahuas and exhibitors alike do not like a human being hulking over the animal. Any reexamination must be done on the table, or with the dog in the exhibitor's arms.

When a Standard is being written by breeders, they should not assume that they do not have to include that which they think everyone knows. Everyone does not know the little details and peculiarities of a breed. *Judges can only judge, and breeders can only breed, by what is written in the Standard.* There are not many breeder-judges of Chihuahuas, nor are there many judges who have ever owned, or shown, a Chihuahua. Thus, it is extremely important to include specific and vital details in the Standard. A case in point is that the present Standard fails to mention the well-defined stop that a Chihuahua must have. This is a very serious omission. Without a well-defined stop the Chihuahua would not have the well-rounded apple-domed head, with the approximate 90-degree angle of the muzzle to the skull.

In judging the Chihuahua by its Standard of Excellence in the show ring, a judge must be very familiar with the Standard itself. Before applying for approval to judge the breed, one should have spent time around the Chihuahua ring observing the dogs. A prospective judge should have discussed the breed with experienced breeders, and have taken opportunities to actually go over young puppies and adult dogs at seminars, shows and matches. From these experiences, plus the words of the Standard, one should be able to form a mental picture of what the ideal Chihuahua should look like. In addition, the judge should be able to extrapolate five or six important breed characteristics that epitomize the breed. Judges must be able to sort out the dogs quickly with these images in mind and be prepared to discuss them, if necessary, after the judging is over. Discussions, however, must be limited to the owner or handler of the dog in question. At all times, the judge is looking at each individual dog, comparing it not only to the Standard, but to other competing specimens. It is a very demanding responsibility and requires extreme concentration. The judge must be secure in an extensive knowledge of the breed and in judging convictions.

Exhibitors, too, have an equal responsibility. They must show only the best-quality Chihuahuas and be prepared to discuss, reasonably and without prejudice, the reasons for showing that particular animal. Whenever exhibitors go into the ring, they must ask themselves, "Would I show this dog in the Bred by Exhibitor Class? Is it a Chihuahua of which I can be proud to say that I am the breeder?" My observation of some specimens that are shown is that many people just look at the head and fail to evaluate the whole dog. They fail to watch the gait, and as a result, some dogs that are shown do not have balance and are not typey, nor are they sound mentally and physically.

On the other hand, some people are just not good handlers. They do not have the ability to coordinate with the dog, nor do they know how to bring out the dog's best characteristics. Poor handling of a dog can ruin the appearance of a really good Chihuahua. Poor handling of an inferior specimen only emphasizes the poor qualities of the dog.

When judging, we must be as careful in selecting the Reserve Winner as in selecting the Winner, for there is always the possibility that the Reserve Winner may move up to the Winner's circle if the winning dog is disqualified at a later date. Of course, judging is purely a subjective matter. Even breeders of long standing and outstanding reputation for top-quality Chihuahuas may not agree in interpretation of the Standard.

During a seminar at the Chihuahua Club of America, nine prominent breeders were asked to evaluate four dogs and place them, in order of quality, one, two, three and four. The results were as follows:

Chihuahua #	Placement	No. of Judges Making Placement
10	1	7
	2	2
	3	0
	4	0
20	1	0
	2	4
	3	3
	4	2
30	1	1
	2	1
	3	2
	4	5
40	1	1
	2	2
	3	4
	4	2

Ear fringe on a Long Coat Chihuahua starts midway and wisps outward.
Terry

Ear fringe on a Papillon is full, starts high and loops over.　　*Terry*

This example has been included to illustrate that, even among breeders, judging is a very subjective thing and 100 percent agreement is not possible.

COMPARISON OF THE LONG COAT CHIHUAHUA AND THE PAPILLON

Casual observers of the Long Coat Chihuahua and the Papillon quite frequently get the two breeds confused, particularly when the Long Coat Chihuahua has markings and color similar to those of a Papillon. However, there are many major differences between these two breeds, and upon close observation one will easily learn to distinguish between them. Some of the major distinctions are as follows:

HEAD
CHIHUAHUA: Well-rounded; apple-domed; breadth between the ears; molera allowed.
PAPILLON: Small; skull of medium width; slightly rounded.
MUZZLE
CHIHUAHUA: Moderately short and slightly pointed.
PAPILLON: Fine; longer with more of a taper; abruptly thinner than the head.
EYES
CHIHUAHUA: Full; set well apart; color in keeping with the color of the dog.
PAPILLON: Medium size; always dark.
TEETH
CHIHUAHUA: Level or scissors.
PAPILLON: Scissors only.
EARS
CHIHUAHUA: Erect ears only; large and flaring at sides with a 45-degree angle when at rest, erect and move higher up on head when alert.
PAPILLON: Dropped ears allowed; rounded tips; larger and more flaring; at 45-degree angle when alert, move in a butterfly fashion.
BODY
CHIHUAHUA: No pronounced tuckup.
PAPILLON: Discernible tuckup.
LEGS
CHIHUAHUA: Forelegs set well under; free play at elbows; hind legs, hocks well let down.
PAPILLON: Forelegs more slender and fine boned in relation to

size; removal of dewclaws on forelegs optional; hind leg dewclaws must be removed.

FEET

CHIHUAHUA: Small toes well split up, neither hare nor cat foot; nails moderately long.

PAPILLON: Thin and elongated so they are harelike.

TAIL

CHIHUAHUA: Moderately long; three tail carriages allowed (up, out, or in a loop over the back with tip just touching the back).

PAPILLON: Long; carried arched over the body with the plume hanging to either side.

COAT

CHIHUAHUA: Flat or slightly curly; undercoat preferred.

PAPILLON: Flat on back and sides of body; no undercoat; more abundant coat and feathering.

EAR FRINGE

CHIHUAHUA: Shorter, wispier; starts lower down on ear.

PAPILLON: Starts higher up on ear; loops over like an upside down U.

COLOR

CHIHUAHUA: Any color that is solid, marked or splashed in any configuration; color of eyes, eye rims and nose in keeping with color of dog.

PAPILLON: Always particolored; color on head must cover both ears back and front and extend without interruption over both eyes; white blaze preferred; symmetry of face marking preferred; nose, eye rims and lips always black.

SIZE

CHIHUAHUA: *Weight* requirements: no minimum, with maximum disqualification.

PAPILLON: *Height* requirements: minimum with no disqualifications; maximum with disqualifications.

In addition to the major differences mentioned above, there are, of course, many degrees of subtle variation between the Long Coat Chihuahua and the Papillon. Continuous observation and study of the two breeds will soon make these subtleties apparent to the eyes of the beholder.

7

Choosing a Chihuahua for Showing, Breeding or Companionship

THE CHIHUAHUA, in many cases, can be the ideal pet. It is small and easy to care for no matter which variety is selected. Its life expectancy is rather long, thus the Chihuahua will provide many years of happy companionship for the family. The breed is very bright and affectionate, and although tiny, makes an excellent watchdog.

With good health care, practiced by at least twice-yearly visits to the veterinarian, many Chihuahuas will live well into the middle teen years and often beyond.

Although the Chihuahua is a sturdy little dog, considering its size it is not a dog for everyone. It cannot be kept out-of-doors in a doghouse. It is very definitely an indoor dog and likes to be kept warm.

It is not a breed for little children, nor for rough-and-tumble people of any age. A dog of this size can easily be seriously injured by an accidental fall from a sofa, or by a very active child falling on top of it during playtime.

The Chihuahua does not need a great deal of exercise. While

large breeds of dogs should be walked daily, the Chihuahua can get all the exercise it needs just by running around the house or apartment. It does enjoy walks outside, though, provided the weather is sunny and warm. It adapts well to most environments and locales.

These little dogs make good family pets provided the owners are very gentle in the art of handling small animals. The Chihuahua has a soft spot at the top of the skull, known as a molera. This is a distinct characteristic of the breed and resembles the soft spot on a human baby's head. The molera should not cause alarm, and it is not a defect. With reasonable care, there is no need to worry about it. For many years, it was thought that the dog was not purebred unless there was evidence of a molera. This is not true, however, for every once in a while this soft spot will close. Generally, in the great majority of dogs, perhaps as many as 90 percent, the opening in the skull does not close. This is one of the reasons that many breeders prefer not to have their dogs go to families with very small and active children.

The Standard for the breed calls for a dog up to six pounds. It is recommended that if you are buying a Chihuahua strictly for a family pet and the family includes children of various ages, it is probably best to select a puppy that will mature closer to the six-pound size.

As soon as the decision is made to buy a Chihuahua puppy, there are also many other decisions to make. Long Coat or Smooth Coat? Male or female? Tiny size or the maximum size? Show puppy? Obedience puppy? Companion puppy? Future breeding puppy? Or, an all-purpose puppy? These are all very serious considerations and must be evaluated very carefully before plunging ahead for that first purchase of a Chihuahua. First and foremost, try to get literature about the breed. Good sources are the Chihuahua Club of America, the American Kennel Club, and if there is one, the local Chihuahua club. There are several regional Chihuahua clubs throughout the country. The AKC will supply you with the name and address of the local club's secretary, as well as the Standard for the breed and a list of available books about the Chihuahua. It is a good idea to read some books about the breed and know the Standard before seeking out a puppy.

In addition to the above organizations, there are hundreds of all-breed clubs scattered throughout the country. These clubs usually have a list of reputable breeders in the area. If there are no breeders nearby, perhaps you could attend a dog show and talk to some

Four-week-old Smooth Coats owned by Trish Lambert, Okatoma Kennels.

Six-week-old Long Coats owned by Susan F. Payne.

breeders there. Breeders travel far and wide to show their dogs, and this is a good place to meet them. The local kennel club or the AKC can advise you as to the dates and locations of such events. Another source of breeder listings is nationally published dog magazines. These can be purchased at most newsstands.

It is desirable to go to a reputable breeder for your puppy. Many times the breeder will have on the premises both sire and dam, and in some cases may even have the grandparents and great-grandparents of the puppy. This gives the prospective puppy buyer an opportunity to judge the approximate size of the dog at maturity, the temperament that it will most likely have and its conformation qualities. You should note the conditions of the kennel, as well as the puppies' health and how the Chihuahuas are cared for.

Whether one is buying a pet puppy, or show/breeding stock, some basic considerations remain the same. Each of us wants a strong, healthy puppy of sound temperament, free of any congenital defects and recognizable as a Chihuahua. Outstanding conformation qualities are of concern only if you are planning to breed and/or exhibit.

A pet puppy may be purchased anytime from eight weeks of age and older. Breeding and show stock is best purchased after six months of age. The puppy you select should be healthy, the eyes bright and clear of any mucous discharge. Occasionally, some Chihuahuas will have little teardrop stains at the inner-eye corner, but if the tear itself is a clear watery fluid, this should be of little concern. Some toy breeds have small tear ducts, so tears may well up, and over, the eyelids, leaving a stain under the eyes. Do not confuse this with a sign of illness, as with mucus coming from the eyes. Dogs that tear-stain early in life most likely will continue to do so throughout their lives. The puppy should be free of parasites, both internal and external. The coat should be soft and glossy, with no dander.

While at the kennel, watch the puppies as they play on the floor for their reaction to each other and to you as a stranger. Before picking up a puppy, let it first look you over. Handle the puppy gently, but firmly and with care. Keep the pup close to your body. No dog likes to be held high up and dangled in the air. Keep a firm, steady grip and do not let the animal jump out of your arms or lap. It is best to sit on the floor to participate in puppy activities.

Depending on age, ears may be up or down. Ears sometimes do not become erect until the puppy is four or five months old. During teething time and up to about six months of age, the ears may go up and down several times in each day.

Puppies should not be thin. Bones must not show. The skin is to cover the body well and show signs of elasticity, as well as be soft to the touch. It should be clean and clear, with no signs of blemishes. The coat should also cover the body well, with no bald spots. There should be no nasal or eye mucous discharge and no diarrhea.

If the prospective buyer is not familiar with the breed, it may be wise to take along a knowledgeable person to help make the selection of a puppy, especially if the puppy is for show and/or breeding.

Remember that Chihuahuas live to a ripe old age. The personality of the puppy must be in harmony with that of the prospective buyer and the family. The whole family should be present. Keep in mind that all puppies are cute, so it is wise to spend some time with the breeder asking many questions as to care, feeding, housing, housebreaking, simple obedience training and grooming.

If the puppy is being purchased as a family pet and companion, each child and/or adult should be involved in the selection and responsibility of care and ownership. Responsibility means that one or more persons must be in charge of feeding, cleaning, exercising, grooming, watering, training, playing with and loving this tiny little companion, who cannot do all these things for himself.

Do not be afraid to buy an older dog if it seems sound in mind and body. It will only take a few days of adjustment if it has an outgoing personality to begin with.

Although the initial cost may seem high, when the cost is divided over the long life span of the Chihuahua, it becomes very little in terms of money. In terms of the love and enjoyment you will receive from your Chihuahua, the cost will be well worth it. Maintenance cost of a Chihuahua is relatively small. A good diet, daily brushing and simple manners training cost little. A minimum of twice-yearly veterinary checkups and booster inoculations as preventive medicine, combined with a little daily exercise and plenty of love, is all it takes to keep your dog healthy and happy. Puppy should be inoculated for distemper, hepatitis, leptospirosis, parvovirus, kennel cough and rabies, as the barest minimums.

When a price is quoted, keep in mind that Chihuahua litters are very small. Veterinary care, which may include a Caesarian section and shipping, as well as stud service, is very costly. Yes, Chihuahuas are small, but you are not buying a puppy by the pound. All expense

Seven-week-old Smooth Coats bred by Brooke Kaye-Albright. Four of these puppies became champions.

Fourteen-week-old Long Coat owned by breeders Mark and Kathy Lenhart.

Ch. RJR's Glamour Reglila at four months of age. Breeder/owners, Ruth Bahlman and Rose Mioduszewski.

factors plus quality must be figured into the cost. The size of the puppy has nothing to do with its cost. It is difficult and costly to raise animals of this size; to bring them up to be happy, healthy, energetic, and loving. Most breeders find it impossible to turn a profit. They raise these little ones because they are caring people who love the breed, and so want to perpetuate and continually improve it for others to love and enjoy as companion pets, or as show/breeding stock.

Do not be surprised if the breeder asks you a great many questions. Where will the puppy live? Are your children gentle with animals? Does your spouse want a dog? This is a very serious question, because of who will end up caring for and tending the dog. Is your yard fenced in? Will the puppy be alone all day? The breeder will be very concerned about where the puppy is going. Breeders want their puppies to have the best possible homes and be cared for with love and concern. Since breeders are responsible for bringing puppies into the world, they want them to go to the most responsible, caring people.

Never give a puppy as a surprise gift. The new owner must be willing to care for it financially and lovingly. The puppy may be with the owner for fifteen years or more. It will require housebreaking and good manners' training. There will be yearly veterinary care, cost of food, dishes, a bed area, perhaps spaying and/or neutering, and various medications and vaccinations to keep it in good health. Owning a dog requires a sense of responsibility. The owner must be willing to train, care for, play with, exercise and love the pet. A surprise gift may be placing too much responsibility upon the person receiving it, thus the pet may be neglected. Dogs have an innate sense of lack of love from humans, and act accordingly. An unloved pet is an unhappy pet.

Do not buy a dog for delivery at Christmas time or any other celebrated holiday. It is too stressful for human and animal alike. Puppy should not be forced into a house of excitement amid the confusion of holiday festivities. It is much better to leave a collar and a leash or a picture under the tree. In addition, Christmas ornaments and wrapping paper can be lethal for your new puppy. Ingestion of an ornament may require surgery for removal. Christmas plants, such as the berries of mistletoe and some trees, can be toxic. The excitement of the holiday may result in injury to your new Chihuahua if a child accidentally falls on it. All in all, it is safer to bring your new pet home after the holiday is over.

Ch. Genbrook Pittore Justin Time at eleven months, won Best in Sweepstakes at the CC of Northern California for breeder/owner, Brooke Kaye-Albright. S. M. "Dick" Dickerson judged. *Callea*

A beautiful three-month-old puppy, Bliss Hoosier Royal Charmer. This Smooth Coat is breeder/owned by Elizabeth J. Bliss.

Whether to buy a male or a female puppy is a question often asked. This should make no difference if you are a responsible person and take your dog rearing seriously. It is no more difficult to housebreak a male than a female. It is all a matter of consistency in your training instructions and carrying them out with your pet. The puppy should be put on a training schedule. It should to be taken out of doors early in the morning, after naps, after playtime, after every meal and, the last time, at night before retiring. Keep in mind that a very young puppy will have to relieve itself many more times than an adult dog. Take puppy to the same spot each time, for faster learning. Keep the area clean. It is your responsibility to clean up after your dog, at your home, at public places and outside of the hotels where you spend your vacations. Be a responsible dog owner and a good dog neighbor.

Spaying or neutering is appropriate for pets. If you want the Chihuahua for loving companionship only, then it is recommended that the female be spayed and the male be castrated. It is less of a problem to deal with as the dog reaches adulthood, and it is better for the health of the animal. It also prevents unwanted pregnancies with females, and may help in keeping the male from wandering. Of course, a dog should not be allowed to roam freely anyway. Free roaming leads to all kinds of injuries, and even death. If spayed or castrated, your pet will remain healthy and happy. You will not be bringing unwanted puppies into the world and you will not be contributing to the many unwanted puppies that are already here.

When buying a purebred Chihuahua puppy, you are entitled to receive AKC eligibility for registration papers. Quoted from the AKC booklet *Dogs—General Information* is advice regarding this matter:

> When you buy a dog represented as AKC registrable, you should receive an AKC dog Registration Application form properly filled out by the seller. When completed by you and submitted to AKC with the proper fee, this form will enable you to register the dog. When the application has been processed, you will receive an AKC Registration Certificate.
>
> Under AKC Rules, any person who sells dogs represented as AKC registrable, must maintain records that make it possible to give full identifying information with every dog delivered even though AKC "papers" are not yet available. Do not accept a promise of later identification.
>
> The Rules and Regulations of the American Kennel Club stipulate

that whenever someone sells or delivers a dog registrable with AKC, the dog must be identified either by putting into the hands of the buyer a properly completed AKC Registration Application or by giving the buyer a bill of sale or written statement, signed by the seller, giving the dog's full breeding information as:

- Breed, sex and color of the dog
- Date of birth of the dog
- Registered names of the dog's sire and dam (with numbers if possible)
- Name of the breeder

Persons who purchase dogs that are represented as being eligible for registration with the American Kennel Club and who encounter problems in acquiring the necessary Registration Application forms should write to the AKC, giving all of the information they received at the time of purchase. The AKC will attempt to assist them in the matter.

Whether you have purchased a puppy for show/breeding or as a pet, before leaving the kennel with your new puppy get a written statement from the breeder stating you have X number of hours—forty-eight hours is reasonable—to take the puppy to your veterinarian for a thorough physical examination. It should also state that if the veterinarian does not find the puppy in generally sound health, you may return it for a full refund. You must pay for the puppy before taking it to your veterinarian. If you injure it in any way while it is in your possession, then you have bought it as a final sale. You are responsible for this puppy from the time you leave the breeder's premises, so use the utmost caution while puppy is in your care. Put the puppy in a crate for safe transportation. You should, of course, have made an appointment with your veterinarian before you go to visit the kennel.

Choosing a Chihuahua for showing and breeding requires even more discernment in selection of a puppy or adult dog. Many breeders think that show stock should also be breeding stock, that one should not be any different from the other. This is sound reasoning, particularly if one is able to keep only a small number of dogs. The teeny-weeny dogs are cute, and certainly showable, but frequently do not have the capacity to become natural-whelping brood bitches, nor much-used stud dogs. So if you are limited in the number of dogs you can maintain, it would be wise to leave the extremely small Chihuahuas, both male and female, for nonbreeders to show and love.

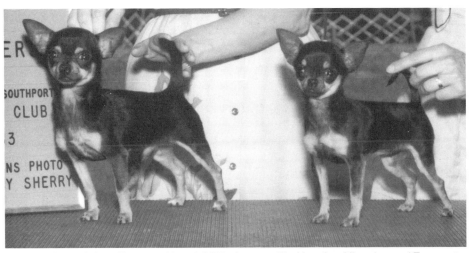

Litter brother and sister, Terrymont Marsubri Chippity, owned by Mary Ann Minervino, and Terrymont Marsubri Tango, owned by James and Susan Payne, winners at the CC of Greater New York. Judge was Geraldine Hess. Both Smooth Coats became champions. Breeders, Marcia Greenburg and Terrymont Kennels. *Gilbert*

When puppies are of high quality, they can finish their championships at an early age. Here is Ch. Vanderpool's Super Blue Star, a Long Coat owned, bred and handled by Veta Vanderpool. *Booth*

91

Everyone into the basket. Here is Trinka, Twinkle and Trinket, ten-week-old Long Coats owned by Millie Williams.

Dear Miss Solitaire and Dear Miss Rain Bow, Long Coat puppies owned by Shirley Dear, Canada.   *Lindt*

As to the age of the puppy purchased for show/breeding stock, it is sensible and less expensive over the long term, and from a quality-assurance viewpoint, to purchase a Chihuahua *not less than six months of age.* By this time, there is ready evidence of normal growth patterns of all the necessary and vital parts. There is indication of size as well as soundness, both mental and physical. Conformation qualities, muscle tone and sturdiness of legs, general good health and charisma needed for the show ring are becoming evident now also. There should be two normal testicles in males and evidence of beginning good adult coat, particularly if it is a Long Coat puppy. It will be less expensive to buy the best now than to be sorry later. By buying a two- to three-month-old puppy, many people think you can save money. There are just too many things that can go wrong with a very young puppy as it matures. For example, testicles may not descend in males, teeth may become misaligned, there may be poor muscle development or poor coat development. There may even be signs of mental or physical disability. A six-month or older puppy will give a much better indication of the dog's appearance at full maturity, only a few months away, than one that is under six months of age.

In addition, the same principles used in purchasing a pet puppy should also be used for purchasing a show/breeding puppy. The same qualities of health and temperament apply here as well; plus, you must look for the conformation qualities more carefully. Front legs must be straight with good bend of stifle on rear legs. General soundness of conformation and mental fitness should be apparent. Coat quality, the all important charismatic personality, trainability, adaptability and so on should all be present to some degree.

The cost of the show/breeding puppy may be considerably more than the pet price. If you deal with a reputable breeder, however, he or she should be fair and honest with you. After all, it is to the breeder's advantage also that you get a quality show/breedable puppy, for every time you enter the ring you will be advertising the breeder's kennel name. Breeders want to be proud of what they have sold you. Their reputation for honesty and fairness is based on how they treat their clients and their dogs. Good relationships between the breeder and client now may mean additional show/breeding puppy sales later.

At the same time, remember that you, too, may be in the seller-breeder's position in the future. Do not make unreasonable demands, particularly as to the cost of the show/breeding puppy. The breeder still has the same expenses, whether one sells a pet puppy or a show dog.

8

How to Groom
a Chihuahua

W HETHER ONE HAS a show dog or a loving pet, basic grooming should be somewhat similar. It will vary only to the degree that the dog is groomed. Good grooming helps keep the dog clean and healthy. With a pet, perhaps there is a little less trimming. Other than that, it makes sense to care for all the vital necessities of bathing, brushing, some trimming and general cleanliness.

Unless a Chihuahua is being shown, it is not necessary to bathe it constantly. In fact, even if it is being shown frequent baths are not necessary. As in many breeds, a few minutes per day of brushing, good diet and proper health care will be all that is necessary to keep the coat and skin clean, shining and healthy.

Grooming must begin with good physical condition, regardless of the age of the Chihuahua, before any actual grooming takes place. No matter how well one grooms a Chihuahua, if the dog is not in good physical condition, little or nothing will be achieved. This is true not only for the pet companion dog, but it is true especially for the show dog. After reviewing the following explanations of good grooming for the show ring, the companion dog owner will be able to choose as much or as little as desired to keep the pet in good condition. Practice the following techniques as much as possible for

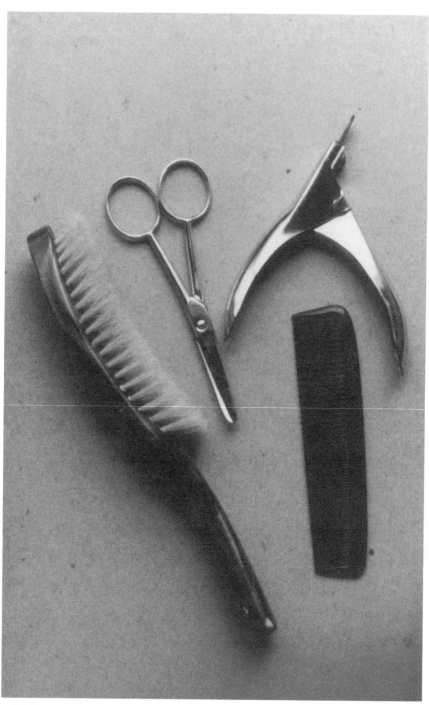

Minimum grooming tools required: long and narrow natural bristle brush; curved, blunt-end scissors; nail clippers; hard rubber comb.

exceptionally good grooming care. As proper grooming contributes to the dog's good health, the healthier the dog, the longer the life span. We all want our beloved Chihuahuas to be around for a long time. The Chihuahua that is in good physical condition will show it in his manner by being alert and sprightly at all times. Pet or show dog, everyone wants a dog that is energetic and happy.

Daily maintenance and grooming of your Chihuahua is a good habit to develop. The dog will look and feel in top condition. Daily grooming will also make last-minute show grooming entirely unnecessary. A little trim here and there, in addition to a bath, will have your dog ready for the show ring in no time flat.

Daily grooming also prevents dog odor. For the unkempt dog, this can become quite strong and even permeate the house. The person living in the house may not notice, as one's nose becomes insensitive to doggie odors when living with the pet for some time. To the visitor, though, this is an entirely different story. If the dog is in a constantly unkempt condition, as soon as newcomers enter your house they will get a strong sense of dog odor. This can occur with just one dog or with several. Of course, the more dogs you have, the more you must pay attention to cleanliness at all times, particularly if the dogs are quartered in the house.

Here is a list of those items needed for good grooming care:

Natural bristle brush
Hard rubber comb
Mild shampoo
Medicated shampoo for
    those with skin or coat
    problems
Creme and/or body rinse
Cotton swabs on plastic
    sticks
Wads of cottonballs

Nail clippers
Thinning shears
Whisker-trimming scissors
Edge-trimming scissors
Toothbrush
Tooth scaler
Blow dryer
Absorbent cotton towels
Old nylon stockings

You will use some or all of these items depending on whether or not you are grooming your dog for the show ring.

If the dog has had daily brushing, and has been on a sensible diet to maintain good health, there will be little to worry about as to shedding. The shedding of the Chihuahua's coat will usually come in the spring, If you breed your female, she will shed within a few weeks after having weaned a litter. Other shedding periods will vary with the climate in which the dog lives. Daily brushing will keep shedding to the barest minimum. Keep in mind, it does not matter if you have Long Coat Chihuahuas or Smooth Coat Chihuahuas, daily brushing is essential to remove the dead hairs. It may not be as noticeable on the Smooth Coat Chihuahua, but those little short hairs easily stick into fabrics you are wearing and are much more difficult to remove from clothing than the long hairs from a coated dog.

While you are indulging in the brushing routine, and it need not take more than a few minutes to accomplish the job, it is wise to be constantly on the lookout for external parasites, such as fleas, ticks and mites. Look as well for any abrasions which may have occurred by being in contact with some sharp or rough objects or foliage if your Chihuahua is outside a great deal. Look for any skin eruptions that may require medical treatment. Check for matted areas in the body coat and in the fringes and other coat furnishings. Look for parasites between the toes, under the leg pits, and in the tiny ear crevices. Run your hands all over the body for the same reasons. This will also provide stimulation for the skin while you are looking for abnormal signs, as well as making the dog enjoy grooming time.

It is essential that this handling and grooming of the Chihuahua begin at a very early age. The touching and caressing of the puppy can begin from day one, but do not overdo it at that age. Once or twice a day, from birth, just cuddle and rub each little puppy. It will become accustomed to being handled and then will show no fear upon being touched by judges who are strangers. This is a neccesity in the show ring.

BRUSHING

Brushing can begin when puppy is about four weeks old. The brushing should take place both on your lap and on the grooming table. Train your puppy to lie down on its back while on your lap and this will make underbelly brushing much easier for both you and your dog. It also facilitates nail clipping. A long narrow brush is better than a wide one, as the narrow brush will be able to get into the smaller areas. Brushing is preliminary to bathing.

Use a long and narrow, natural bristle brush. A natural bristle brush and a hard rubber comb will prevent static shocks, especially during dry weather when there is little humidity. Place puppy on its back and gently go over the underbelly, stroking downward toward

Nail trimming is easily accomplished if the dog has been trained to lie down in your lap.

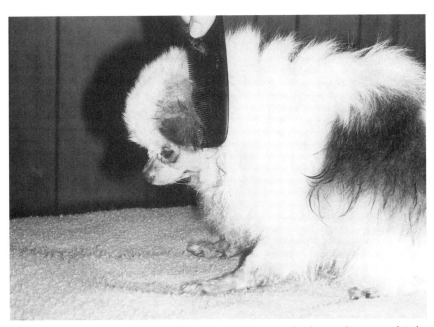

A hard rubber comb is good for the fringe. It prevents static shock sometimes associated with dry weather.

the rear. This will not take long, as even on a Long Coat Chihuahua there is not excessive hair on the underbelly.

For the remainder of the coat and furnishings, place your puppy on a nonskid sturdy table top and begin brushing slowly and gently in the same direction that the hair is growing. There should be several strokes during the next stage, in which you brush in the opposite direction to which the hair is growing. This will ensure that the dead hair is removed. The final body coat brushing, the third stage, is to go back to brushing in the direction the coat is growing. Pay careful attention to mats, which should be removed gently by parting the hairs a few at a time. If you should accidentally hurt your dog during the grooming process, talk to him kindly, sweetly and soothingly. An extra pat or caress will help, especially if you cradle the dog in your arms at this time. It will be reassuring and make the grooming experience more pleasant. Do not shout or reprimand in any way if you have hurt your dog. Shouting and punishment will only make puppies dislike the grooming process and may very well make them run in the opposite direction when they see the grooming tools coming their way.

Doing some of the grooming on the table also prepares puppies for the show ring, where the examination will be conducted on a table. Always make this an enjoyable time for both you and your dog.

NAIL TRIMMING

Nail trimming should begin while the puppy is only a few days old, as many puppies are born with nails quite long. It can be easily accomplished by having your puppy lie on its back in your lap. With your thumb on the foot pads and your forefinger at the top of the foot opposite the thumb, gently press thumb and forefinger together, just enough so that the toes spread apart. This will make it easier to trim the hook off the end of the dog's nails. Be sure to take off only a little of the nail at a time. When you begin to see the little circle in the center of the end of the nail get larger, you are now approaching the quick, which will bleed if you cut too closely. The AKC Standard calls for a moderately long nail, although many breeders shorten the nails somewhat more than what is called for.

There are two most common types of nail clippers, one oval shaped and one that cuts a more circular shape. Use whichever is most comfortable for you to handle. Some people like to use a file, regular or electric, but the noise may be disturbing to your Chihuahua and could frighten a puppy.

If you should accidentally cut the nail too short and it bleeds, have some kind of styptic preparation ready to clot the blood immediately. This comes in powder and solid forms.

TRIMMING AND THINNING

While the dog is lying on its back on your lap, it is time to trim the long hairs that are growing between the pads on a Long Coat Chihuahua. Use only a curved and blunt-end small scissors, with the curved portion curving away from the underfoot or pads. Trim very carefully, so as not to cut the pad. All the while you are trimming the dog's pad hairs, talk sweetly and gently.

The feathering around the ears on a Long Coat Chihuahua and around the legs, pants and tail is more easily cared for with a hard-rubber comb. This is preferable to a metal comb, which may cause static shocks, as does the use of a nylon brush. These furnishings are usually of a very fine texture and more prone to matting than other sections of the coat. You may want to trim away some of the hair growing inside the ear, but not outside. Keeping the inside ear free of hair will also give a larger look to the ear. In other words, heavily coated ears inside and outside may make the ear appear to be smaller than it is. Trimming the ear is a matter of preference. However, there are many breeders and judges, including the author, who prefer little or no trimming even on a Long Coat Chihuahua. Before doing any ear trimming, place a small wad of cotton inside the ear so that hair will not get into the ear canal.

When finding a mat, gently pry the hairs apart a few at a time. It will take a little longer than the use of a mat splitter, but you will not break or lose any of the long fringes that are desired if you take the time to split the mats by hand. On the tail, where the hair is more profuse, the brush may be used in addition to the comb.

If the pants are of exceptionally thick growth, you may want to use a thinning shears, but do not cut them shorter. Long pants are desirable, but may be thinned only to prevent the dog from appearing too long in body.

Trimming of facial whiskers and eyebrows is a highly controversial subject. There are those who are vehemently opposed to whisker trimming, stating that these are natural feelers for the dog

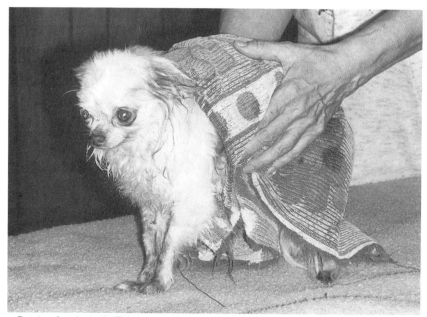

Pat dry after the bath. This takes out excess water and prepares for the next drying stage.

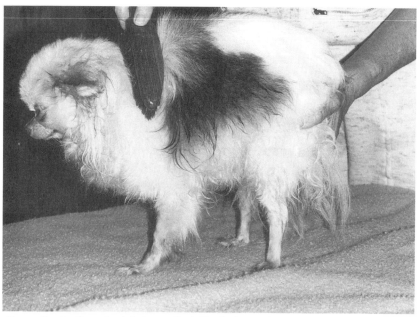

Preparation for the natural drying method. The body coat is brushed in the direction it is growing. The ruff is brushed downward.

and should not be removed under any condition. This subject of whisker trimming, however, pertains only to the show dog. Your decision may be dictated by the shape of your dog's head and/or muzzle. Narrow muzzles should retain the whiskers, to give the illusion of a wider muzzle. In the case of eyebrows, though, if the brow hairs are curling inward toward the eye, they must be cut off. Eventually, hairs that continuously scrape against the eyeball will cause injury to the eye itself.

Hair between the toes and around the foot pads should be removed, to prevent splayed feet. Long hair at the toes should be left on, according to the Standard, although some exhibitors do cut it off.

The stray hairs on the ruff, rump and belly may be trimmed for neatness only.

Nothing should be done to the tail, on either Long Coat or Smooth Coat Chihuahuas. The more full and long a plume on a Long Coat, the better. The Smooth Coat tail should be left flat and furry. Remember, also, that the Smooth Coat should have a ruff on the neck, so do not cut it off. The neck ruff is first brushed downward and then the edge of the ruff is brushed up and outward to form a halo to frame the face.

BATHING

If a Chihuahua has had daily grooming from birth, frequent bathing is not needed unless the dog carries some kind of odor. Daily brushing will help to keep your pet clean and odor free, and will provide a soft and glossy coat. But there will be times when a bath is absolutely necessary, in order to keep it in outstanding condition. A few precautions must be taken during the bath time. It is essential that no water, soap or shampoo get into the eyes or ears. A very mild shampoo should be used. The shampoo may be one that is formulated especially for dogs, or you may use a mild baby shampoo. If your dog has any kind of skin or hair problems, there are shampoos formulated for various specific problems. Check the labels and directions carefully before using any shampoo or conditioner on your dog's coat.

Before bathing the dog, cotton wads should be placed in its ears. The water should be lukewarm. Test it on your wrist before applying it to the dog. To bathe, begin at the front of the dog and wet the coat thoroughly all over, being careful of eyes and ears. Work the shampoo gradually into the coat on top, underneath and toward the rear of the dog, gently massaging all over as you work the shampoo into the coat. Also work the shampoo into the furnishings of ruff, leg fringe, pants and tail plume. Rinse thoroughly. Shampoo left in the coat will dry it out, causing skin problems and dandruff. It will also leave a dull finish on the coat.

If your Long Coat Chihuahua has a flyaway coat—that is, a coat that stands away from the body—try a creme and body rinse as a final step. This, coupled with the nylon stocking method of drying (see below), will help the coat to lie flat against the body when it is dry.

Drying the Coat

Thick all-cotton terry towels are very good for pat drying and getting out the excess water as quickly as possible. These towels are very absorbent. This may be followed by a rubdown massage, which will help to dry the coat and stimulate the skin. Then brush the coat in the direction it is growing. If the dog is excessively wet, you may continue drying with a blow dryer, but check for temperature of the dryer continually, to prevent accidental burns of coat or skin. While you are using the dryer, you must use it so the air is blowing in the direction that the hair is growing, and continually brush at the same time in the same direction. This will keep the coat flat against the body. Blowing in the opposite direction from which the hair is growing will make the body coat stick out. Do not aim the dryer at the dog's face, and do not overdry. Too much heat will dry out the coat and skin and cause considerable problems to both.

If your Long Coat Chihuahua has a flyaway coat, or one that stands out from the body instead of lying flat or slightly curly as called for in the Standard, you will have to go to another method of drying. After having used the creme and body rinse in the final bath stage, and all the appropriate rinsing has been done, dry the dog with soft and thick cotton terry-cloth towels as much as possible. Brush the coat and furnishings in the direction that the coat is growing. *Do not blow dry* if your dog has a flyaway coat. Here is where you will use an entirely different method of drying. You are going to let the dog's coat dry naturally.

Begin by cutting up an old, sheer women's nylon stocking, making it the length of the dog, including the neck, all the way to the end of the rump. Cut holes in the material for the neck, front legs

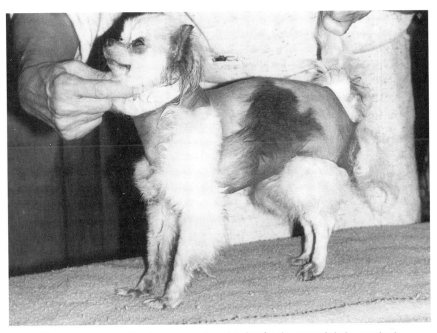

The nylon stocking has been placed on the dog for the natural drying method.

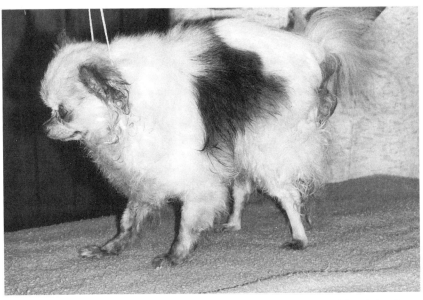

The nylon stocking has been removed; dog is three-quarters dry. The remaining drying time will be without the stocking cover. Note the flat, close-to-the-body coat that has not yet been fully brushed.

Beautifully groomed is Ch. Apoco Deodar Royal Suit, five years old, owned by Trudy Kimball.

only, and tail. If a male, cut an opening for the end of the penis. When you have removed the excess water from the coat and brushed the coat in the proper direction, place this previously prepared nylon body covering onto the dog and let the coat dry naturally. This will take quite a long time. Remove the nylon stocking covering in about three hours and once again brush the coat in the direction it is growing. The coat will now be dry enough to leave off the nylon covering and to continue the natural air drying. You will find that when the coat is dry, even a flyaway coat will cling quite close to the body. This has been accomplished by a combination of things. The creme and body rinse, the fabricated covering, the natural drying, along with the directional brushing, have all combined to bring about a close-fitting body coat.

Finishing

Once your dog is thoroughly dry using either method, there may be some final preparations you will prefer to use. A final rub-down with a finishing glove may help to give added sheen to the coat. On white areas, you may use a cornstarch-based powder, or chalk for added whitening effect, but keep in mind that this must be thoroughly removed by brushing before entering the ring. There must be no evidence of any artificial substance left in the coat when you enter the show ring.

Most of the aforementioned grooming techniques apply to the Long Coat Chihuahua, particularly in the area of trimming. Many breeders promote no trimming whatsoever, preferring to have the Chihuahua in its most natural state. Others prefer to trim, sometimes to excess and to the judge's consternation. These breeders will even go so far as to trim the ruff, the tail and the little area at the end of the rump on a Smooth Coat. The finishing touches will be left up to you—the exhibitor—for the final judgment as to how much trimming is done.

At left is Ch. Judy's Roxanne Robin with Ch. Judy's Bridgette Robin, CDX. Breeder/owner, Judith Dickhaus. With proper home health maintenance such as these dogs have received, your Chihuahua should provide you with enjoyable companionship for many years to come.

9

Home Health
Maintenance

KEEPING AN EYE on your Chihuahua's health on a daily basis may prevent future costly veterinary bills. This chapter focuses on three areas where attention will not only help to keep your pet/show dog healthy, but will also give you many added years of enjoyment from your companion.

EYES

Just wiping around the eyes with a mild boric acid solution will do no harm and will help to keep them clean, especially if there are tear stains in evidence. Chihuahua eyes generally require little care.

EARS

A cotton swab on a soft plastic stick may be used to clean out dirt and wax that you can see. Do not stick anything inside the ear canal. If you cannot see the area to be cleaned, do not probe. If there is no odor coming from the ear, it is likely in good condition. If a foul odor is present, then medical attention is required. For dry ears, a little baby oil may be rubbed in. Dryness at the ear edge of a Smooth Coat is not unusual, especially with aging. For the dog that is constantly turning the head, cocking the head or scratching the ear, have the veterinarian check for ear mites.

TEETH

What may seem like a silly idea may well be the most beneficial for your Chihuahua. Keeping the teeth clean should be done not by periodic visits to the veterinarian, where anesthesia must be used in preparation for scaling and polishing, but by brushing the teeth with a soft, pliable baby's toothbrush three times a week. There is no need to use toothpaste, although there are commercial preparations on the market. A little lukewarm water and thorough brushing a few times each week will keep your dog's teeth sparkling clean. If this is not done, regular scaling with a dental instrument will be necessary to keep your Chihuahua's teeth healthy. Dogs do not like scaling any more than humans do. The easiest approach to good dental health, and by far the least costly, is just plain brushing. You will be pleasantly surprised to find that your Chihuahuas will most likely retain their teeth well into middle age and beyond with this method.

As your puppy is going into adulthood, it is best to keep a careful watch on the formation of the secondary teeth. Sometimes the baby or deciduous teeth do not fall out at the proper time. If you do not keep checking, you may find that one day your show puppy has a double set of teeth! This will require removal of those baby teeth, under anesthesia, by your veterinarian. If the baby teeth are not removed at the proper time, you may find that the alignment of the secondary teeth has been impaired. So keep a careful watch as your puppy is going through the teething stages, especially between the ages of two months to seven months. Full dentition consists of forty-two permanent teeth: twelve incisors, six up and six down; four canines, two up and two down; sixteen pre-molars, eight up and eight down; ten molars, four up and six down. If any teeth are missing, they will most likely be pre-molars. In hairless breeds, the pre-molars are often missing.

A word of caution. Do not remove any deciduous or baby teeth until the particular secondary tooth has erupted, even if only barely.

There have been instances where the secondary teeth have failed to come in when the baby teeth were removed too early.

Whether you have a pet or a show dog, if the same procedures for grooming, bathing, trimming, brushing, nail and teeth care, exercise and diet are followed, your puppy will grow to be a happy and healthy Chihuahua and will remain a loving and devoted part of your family for a great many years.

Am./Can./Bda. Ch. Brecon's Blackadot is proof that good veterinary care can enable a Chihuahua to live a long and healthy life.

10

The Veterinarian's Role

MANY PEOPLE CONSIDER their pets members of the family. Pets are not only tended to physically, but they are played with, traveled with, worried about and cared for when they are ill. It is only natural that the owner should take as much care in selecting a veterinarian as in choosing a family doctor. Keep in mind that in addition to standard veterinary medicine, there are many veterinarians who include holistic medicine, acupuncture, and chiropractic techniques in their practices.

Do not wait until the dog is ill to find a veterinarian. If the dog is seriously injured, time is of the essence. This difficult period is no time to foist a stranger upon the dog, a stranger who will prod, poke and inject with medications. The dog will be under stress from injury or illness, and that alone is enough to frighten it. During the examination, your presence will help to calm the dog, and you can see how the veterinarian handles the animal and how the dog responds to the veterinarian. The owner should be allowed in the examining room and the treatment discussed. This is the time to ask questions about the diagnosis, the treatment done in the office and follow-up to be done at home.

If you are planning to breed, the veterinarian should be willing to be awakened at any hour of the night for emergency treatment or for a Caesarian section at the animal hospital.

If the dog requires hospitalization, under what conditions will he be kept? Is the hospital clean and orderly? Do the medical attendants like animals, or is it just another job? The location of the animal hospital is important, for it must be close enough, especially for emergencies. For regular visits, note the office hours so you can get there before or after your work day.

If this is a routine visit for inoculations or checkup, the owner has some responsibility. Have your dog on a lead at all times in the waiting room. The dog must be under control; it should not be sniffing other animals, nor lunging, growling or snapping. It should have good sanitary manners. Before the visit, write down everything you want to ask about, otherwise you might forget when you get to the office. Know your dog's history, especially if this is a first time visit.

Discuss the fees frankly. Ask if cash is required beforehand or if charge cards are acceptable.

Be certain your dog and your veterinarian are compatible and react well to one another. This is especially crucial in times of stress or emergencies. If the animal and veterinarian do not get along, change veterinarians. After all, if you did not get along with your own doctor, a change would be in order.

PARASITES

Internal and external parasites are not uncommon among dogs living together, or even in a one-dog household. In most cases, parasites can be controlled and/or eliminated if one works at it constantly and diligently. Listed below are some of the most common parasites associated with dogs.

Roundworms. A puppy with roundworms will be thin, but will appear to have a full-rounded belly. The pup may be weak and have diarrhea or a poor coat, even for a puppy. Adult roundworms are long and thin and may reach a length of several inches.

Hookworms. Although smaller than roundworms, they are much more dangerous because they suck blood from the dog's intestine, and puppies can die as a result.

Whipworms are two or three inches long and live in the bowels. Puppies with whipworms are thin, have diarrhea, are anemic and usually appear to be sickly.

Roundworms, hookworms and whipworms all require strict sanitation and periodic worming.

114

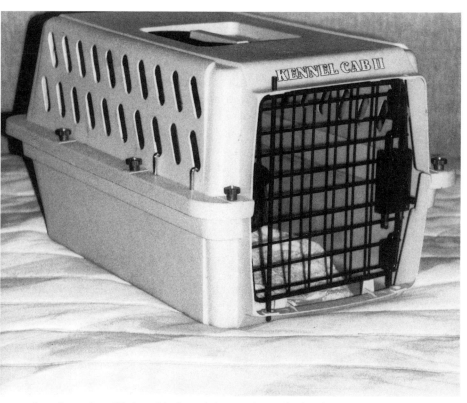

A carrier such as this is an ideal way to transport an animal to the veterinarian's office.

Tapeworms can cause either diarrhea or constipation. As the dog loses nutrients to the tapeworm, he frequently will show a marked increase in appetite.

All worming medications can be hazardous to your dog's health. Medication dosage for worms has to be in ratio to the puppy's weight. Use cautiously and in consultation with your veterinarian.

Heartworm. Although this is a preventable disease, more and more cases seem to appear each year, primarily due to owner neglect in having yearly veterinary checkups. Heartworm can be fatal if not treated. Adult heartworms can be over a foot long and look like spaghetti. If not found in time, they can lead to heart failure or damage other organs such as lungs, kidneys and liver. Symptoms may be a cough, weight loss, breathing problems, and not wanting to participate in playful activities. The mosquito is the culprit that transmits heartworm larvae from dog to dog. A dog must have a blood test before administering heartworm medication. Improper medication can lead to death. Since the medication comes in several forms, it should not take long to find one that is easy to administer.

It is not difficult to give your dog oral medication. For pills, hold open the upper jaw with one hand, open the lower jaw and hold the pill with the other hand and place the pill at the center base of the tongue. Close the dog's mouth immediately and lift the head upward. The dog will swallow naturally. If the pill or tablet is large, cut it in half for easier swallowing and/or stroke the dog's throat while you hold the mouth closed.

For liquids, place medication in an eye dropper or syringe and insert it at the corner of the mouth. Hold head upward, release the liquid and the dog will swallow.

FLEAS

Many people do not realize that fleas can kill newborn puppies if the infestation is very high. Flea residue causes itching, rashes and allergies and can cause anemia. A dog with an allergy to fleas will show signs of baldness, with red and itchy skin. A really acute case can kill a young puppy. One flea can lay hundreds of eggs, which hatch in one week and become adults in about nine days. Fleas have great jumping ability, so can reach the tallest pet. Fleas are survivors; it is difficult to get rid of them.

If using a dip, read the directions carefully. Many products are lethal for young animals. It does not matter how much you spray, dip or powder your pet, you will not get rid of fleas unless you also attack them inside and outside your house. Inside the house you can steam clean the carpets, spray the baseboards and then use a fogger. Outside, keep the lawn mowed and remove all piles of brush and leaves, or other debris. Spray everywhere with an insecticide every ten to fourteen days. Spray at least two or three times.

Do not deflea expectant mothers prior to whelping, nor very young puppies. Checking at least weekly for external parasites will avoid future problems.

TICKS

The **common dog tick,** an eight-legged creature, is a blood-thirsty little beast and can literally bleed a young puppy to death. Adult dogs can become anemic from the common tick, because, if undetected, the tick does not fall off until it becomes engorged with the dog's blood.

The dog must be examined frequently for ticks, before they cause serious harm. Once the tick's probe is embedded in the skin, it is very difficult to remove. If the tick is pulled out, the probe can remain under the skin and cause infection. Try spraying the tick first with a tick spray or alcohol. This may weaken it enough so that it will release its hold. Then remove slowly and carefully. Kill the tick by crushing it. Ticks' favorite hiding places on the dog are behind the ears, between the toes and under the leg pits, although you may also find them on the body of the dog. From the common dog tick, humans can come down with Rocky Mountain spotted fever. Symptoms are fever, headache and skin rash. This disease responds well to antibiotics.

The very tiny, almost microscopic, **deer tick** is responsible for Lyme disease. Symptoms are flu-like, with fever, headache, skin rash, dizziness and sometimes arthritic-like pain in joints. Some symptoms appear within a couple days, others months later. This disease is treated with antibiotics. Tufts University, in Massachusetts, has developed the first diagnostic serum test for Lyme disease, which allows for much earlier diagnosis, thus preventing nerve damage, heart problems and arthritis. The old test required six hours of laboratory time and was expensive. The new test requires only thirty minutes and is very inexpensive.

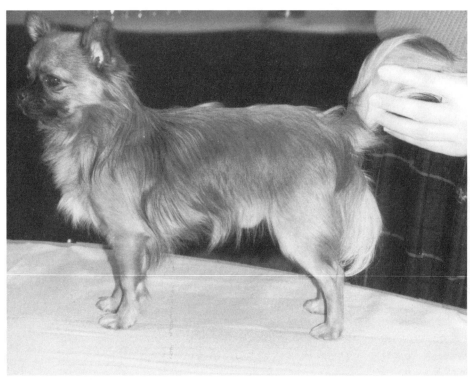

Sudor's Carbon Copy has been trained to stand for examination. This is valuable help for the veterinarian in order to make a proper diagnosis.

MITES

There are several types of mites, but the most common found on dogs are **ear mites,** microscopic creatures usually found in the ear canal. Head shaking and ear scratching are the symptoms. Medicated drops in the ear canal can solve the problem.

The **demodex mite** lives just beneath the dog's outer skin and causes loss of hair in patches. In most cases, these spots can be cured with medicated ointment. The condition is not contagious.

The **sarcoptic mite** causes severe itching and is contagious, but once diagnosed with a skin scraping can be treated with a mange dip. There is some new research being done with an oral medication.

If any mites exist in the kennel, or home, it is best to dip all the dogs, whether or not they have mites.

IMPACTED ANAL GLANDS

Not caused by a parasite, but an annoying problem just the same, is impacted anal glands. There is one sac on each side of the rectum. These sacs sometimes become engorged or even infected and can be very painful. A common symptom is the dog that drags his rear end along the ground. These sacs can be emptied with proper hand manipulation. If it becomes a very frequent problem, the glands can be surgically removed.

PARVOVIRUS

Agri Tech Systems of Portland, Maine, has a new ten-minute test for quickly diagnosing parvovirus. Veterinarians are now able to begin immediate treatment for this troublesome virus. Previously, there was a wait of several days before getting parvo test results. This new test is called the CITE Parvovirus Test. It should save many dogs' lives by quick and correct diagnosis of the parvovirus, which can kill dogs in only a few days.

GERIATRICS

Care of the old dog will vary with each breed. While a giant breed may be considered old at ten years, it is not unusual for the

Chihuahua, with proper care and diet, to live well into the teens and beyond.

Older dogs will need less food, and a different kind of food, because they are less active and may have some physical problems. Many commercial dog food companies have food formulated and specially blended for the older dog.

It is essential as older dogs slow down that they not be allowed to get fat. Obesity will shorten the life span to a considerable degree. They may lose their teeth and require a softer food.

As dogs slow down, so does eyesight dim and hearing fade. They are less active, cannot run up and down the stairs and spend more and more time sleeping on a soft, warm blanket out of drafts. Dogs can be subject to many of the old-age illnesses that humans are. More frequent veterinary consultations may be necessary.

It is vital at this stage that they be given extra consideration and kindness. They should still be kept clean and will most likely still enjoy a daily brushing. They should have a warm and comfortable resting area, but should still engage in some form of walking or play exercise, even though it will not be as long or as strenuous as in younger days. Above all, they will require lots of love and gentle care and will adore being with their human family for longer periods of time.

Eventually, the day will come when your dog can no longer cope with the day-to-day activities because of serious illness, pain or immobility. Now is the time to make the decision, as painful as it might be, to have the dog euthanized.

The author recommends that you make the necessary preparations with your veterinarian in advance, but do not prolong your agony by scheduling the appointment weeks ahead. Do not turn your beloved, aged friend over to a stranger. Hold him in your arms and talk to him as the veterinarian proceeds with the injection. As painful as it is for the owner, your companion's last moments will be in comfort and love as he is held in your arms.

11

Diet

THE GENERAL CARE of your Chihuahua is rather like that of other breeds, but with some variations simply because of the breed's tiny size. Small size should not be mistaken for frailty and delicateness. If cared for nutritionally, handled lovingly, trained gently, groomed expertly and exercised regularly, the Chihuahua can be a solid, happy, well-adjusted breed, ready to adapt to most locales, environments, living quarters and families.

While small in size, the Chihuahua abounds in energy and will require more food per body weight than any giant breed, although the amount may seem small when looked at in the dish. Proper maintenance, for less gorging and enlargement of the stomach, includes the Chihuahua being fed twice daily, even as an adult. The total minimum amount will equal the volume of the entire head and muzzle. This is divided into two meals, one in the morning and one in the evening. One dog may eat a little more, another a little less. Keep in mind at all times that each dog is an individual, so the amount of food will vary from dog to dog. This described portion size is only a guideline. If the Chihuahua is a picky eater, the blame usually rests with the new owner, who most likely failed to carry out the breeder/seller's feeding instructions.

Do not skimp on quality or quantity of food. Trying to manipulate the mature size of the dog through diet is unhealthy and unwise.

Underfeeding to produce tininess will only result in sickly dogs and perhaps even death. The final size of a dog is best left to be determined by the dog's genes.

Individual breeders have definite opinions about what is considered a proper diet. Some even go so far as to cook for their dogs. Many years ago, it was necessary for breeders to concoct and blend nutritious food and to cook these mixtures for dogs in kennels or at home. Finding the correct mixture for maintaining healthy animals required a great deal of time, expense and experimentation.

It is not necessary to do this today. The largest pet food companies spend hundreds of thousands of dollars every year on research as to the best ways and ingredients to feed our dogs. All these dog foods are constantly being tested on canines raised in kennels owned or maintained by the dog food manufacturers. The dogs are under the constant supervision of veterinarians. When improvements are needed or recommended, the research teams go into action. Therefore, it is not necessary to go to all the time, trouble and expense of making food for one's own dogs.

For optimum results and good health, stay with a well-known company and brand name of dog food, particularly those companies that do constant research on the quality of their foods, rather than with a generic brand.

Check the ingredients on the label of the dog food you intend to buy. Make certain that it contains all that is necessary for an active, healthy puppy. The food should not only maintain him during puppyhood, but assist in growth toward a sound adult specimen both mentally and physically. The ingredients in dog food, both dry and canned, are listed on the packages. They include the meat, by-products, vitamins and recommended daily allowance requirements by weight of animal. Directions for use are included, making it very easy for show and pet owners alike.

USE OF VITAMINS AND OTHER SUPPLEMENTS

This is a highly controversial subject. Many breeders feel that if a high-quality name-brand dog food is used, then vitamins and mineral supplements are not needed. This is predicated on whether or not the dog is a good eater. If the animal is finicky, or does not eat the required amount for its size and build, then it may be necessary to introduce vitamins and minerals into the diet. In addition, a pregnant bitch will require additional nutritional supplements.

It must be stressed that it is possible to poison an animal by overdosing with vitamins and minerals. More harm than good can come of introducing too much or too little of any supplement. As with all vitamins and minerals, an overdose can cause considerable damage to bones, tissues and organs. Discuss each individual case with your veterinarian as to the need for nutritional supplements. Read all labels carefully, and administer products by the weight of the animal.

With regard to additional supplements of vitamins and minerals, it is this author's opinion that if a dog is fed a well-balanced diet and is getting a normal amount of exercise per day, it is not necessary to supplement the food, unless the bitch is pregnant, nursing puppies, or is under some kind of stress. If, however, as a pet owner, you are feeding mainly table scraps, then the addition of nutritional supplements is a must.

WHAT TO FEED

Feeding table scraps or treats can also lead to a dog's becoming an unhealthy, finicky eater. Once your puppy is home, you must begin good nutritional habits and feed as recommended by the breeder. A good-quality dry food should be provided as a basic diet and some canned meat may be added if desired. One meal should consist of dry food only, so that the dry food can be crunched against the teeth while eating. This will help to keep the teeth in good, clean condition. The other meal may also consist of dry food that has been moistened with hot water—this may form a gravy in some brands—and canned meat may be added. When the water has cooled, stir the mixture and feed. Meals should be at the same time each day.

At no time should you change the dog's diet abruptly. Gradually introduce the new brand of food you have chosen, using a little less of the other food and a little more of your new brand each day, until the dog has been successfully weaned full time to the new brand of food. A gradual change in diet will prevent such ailments as diarrhea or upset stomach, and will also keep the dog from becoming finicky.

A young puppy will eat much more than an adult dog, in proportion to its size. A puppy that is five weeks old will eat about five meals per day. A two-month-old will eat four meals per day; a four- to six-month-old, three meals per day. When the puppy is six to seven months of age, he will most likely be ready for an adult portion and two meals daily. These are approximate ages for decreasing the number of meals. If a puppy is eating all that it is given, it is not ready to go to the next stage of fewer meals and larger portions. If he is leaving much of the food at each meal, he is most likely ready to go to the next stage of one less meal and larger portions per day. Moistened food should be lukewarm, not hot.

Some dogs will have different nutritional requirements, such as those that are pregnant and/or nursing puppies; those that may have a kidney or heart problem; those that are overweight (as many pets are); or those that have allergies of the skin or coat. These dogs require special diets. There are foods that are commercially made for these particular needs. Consult your veterinarian before using special foods.

HOW MUCH TO FEED

Body conformation has something to do with the amount of weight a dog carries. Some dogs are lean and rangy, while others are prone to heftiness. Both types resemble human counterparts.

As in humans, obesity in dogs may be caused by a genetic factor. If the parents and/or grandparents tended toward obesity, there is a good chance this will be passed on to the puppies. The same holds true for lean, lanky or rangy dogs. Common sense in feeding can help to alleviate these conditions, although it may not completely solve the problems.

For the obese animal, it is necessary to cut back on caloric intake by reducing the quantity of food or by using a food specifically formulated for obesity. Exercise is an important factor here. Lack of exercise contributes greatly to the increase in fat globules. Of course, the fatter the dog gets, the less likely the dog will exercise, preferring to sit on the couch or lounge around the house all day. In this case, it will be necessary to participate in your dog's exercise program. It will be good for both of you. Go for walks each day. Keep in mind, though, that the exercise must be introduced gradually. A dog that has been lying around the house for years cannot take a five-mile walk on the first day. If you are huffing and puffing and your cardiovascular system is not in good shape, think of what it is like for your little dog. It will take several months of daily walking to bring your dog back to normal condition. It is easier for humans to control a dog's diet than their own, particularly because the human has the keys to the refrigerator. When your dog slims down, you might even thank him for getting you back in shape!

Many dog foods today are produced for various stages of life: the growing puppy, the adult dog, the older dog, the obese dog and the less active dog. Each of these foods has been carefully calibrated for a particular purpose. Read the labels carefully before feeding to your dog. Some foods may even state that they are for occasional use only and not to be used as a steady diet. Usually these kinds of foods are treats of some kind.

Directions for amount to feed are on the labels. Usually listed by the dog's weight or activity, these directions are only a guideline. Each dog is an individual and must be fed accordingly.

Getting a lean dog fatter is just as difficult as getting a fat one thinner. If the puppy is overactive, he may need a higher-quality protein, as well as an increase in caloric values. Feeding several small meals per day will increase the amount of food and calories without making the puppy feel overly full all the time. If your dog's ribs show, he is most likely too thin. If you cannot feel his ribs with pressure, he is probably too fat. Maintain the same diet and the same feeding hours each day. This will lead to fewer digestive tract upsets.

Occasionally a dog will go off his feed for a day or so. If he appears to be healthy, runs around, drinks a normal amount of water, sleeps and plays normally, has no discharge from eyes or nose, and is normal in every other respect, there is most likely nothing wrong with him. If lack of appetite persists for more than two or three days, seek veterinary help.

A stud dog should not be fed just prior to using him at stud. It is better to wait until after servicing and then serve only a light meal. A dog that is constantly used at stud should be kept in peak condition and the diet should be a highly nutritious one. Constant servicing may require additional vitamin and mineral supplements.

The brood bitch, if on two meals a day, should go to three meals per day at least by her fifth week of pregnancy, but should not get so much food that she will get excessively fat. A slight increase in calcium, as well as vitamins A and D, would be advised at this time and throughout nursing. One of the commercially well known substitutes for mother's milk, such as Esbilac, may also be given throughout gestation. It is also good for weaning puppies.

Clean and fresh water should be available for all dogs at all times.

Dishes should be of material that puppies cannot chew and of a size they cannot fall into. At left is a water dish to hang on a crate while traveling. At right is a dish for an adult dog's food and at lower center is a puppy feeding bowl, small and shallow. All are stainless steel.

BODY BUILDERS

In order for a dog to achieve optimum growth and energy potential, its food must contain nutrients that are usable by the dog in amounts sufficient for each stage of life.

A dog's diet should contain **protein** for bone growth and tissue healing. **Carbohydrates** are a common nutrient in many dog foods, are a good source of energy and are thought to be needed for reproduction and lactation. **Fats** will tone the skin and keep the coat shiny. Excess fat is stored under the skin, so one must be careful of the amount given. Too much fat will result in an obese dog; too little will result in a shivering dog, as he will have little fat protection from the cold. As in humans, it is better to have polyunsaturated fats rather than animal fats in the diet.

Calcium and **phosphorous** are needed for bone growth, tooth formation and a normal nervous system. Without a balance of these two minerals, bone diseases can occur. Calcium is also needed for muscles, nerve functions and blood clotting. These two minerals are usually combined. An overdose of calcium can cause bone disease in young animals, as well as kidney ailments. **Vitamin D** is used in conjunction with these two minerals for quicker absorption into the system.

Magnesium is for the nervous system. Lack of magnesium can lead to seizures.

Manganese is sometimes confused with magnesium. Manganese is for reproduction, bone and cartilage growth and the pituitary gland. **Zinc** is for good coat and healthy skin. It promotes the healing of wounds and is used in treatment for skin diseases. It is also an important component of both immunity and growth. **Iodine** is for the thyroid. **Potassium** and **sodium** are utilized together for fluid balance.

Iron combines with B_{12}, protein and copper and is for hemoglobin to carry oxygen throughout the blood. **Selenium** is for the heart and immune system. Research indicates it may help in the prevention of cancer.

Vitamin A is needed for good skin and coat, as well as for eyesight and normal growth. It is usually combined with **Vitamin D.** **Vitamin B** is for coat, skin, eyes and the nervous system. **Vitamin C** aids in healing of body tissue and for the blood. It is thought to be effective in battling bacterial infections and for the relief of allergies. **Vitamin D** is necessary for proper growth of bones. Lack of this vitamin can cause bone deformity. **Vitamin E** is commonly referred to as the "fertility" vitamin. It is found abundantly in wheat germ. Although it has not been scientifically proven, many breeders feel that, by feeding wheat germ or some other form of vitamin E, they have more virile stud dogs, more lively and energetic puppies and fewer aborted litters.

12

What Every Chihuahua Owner Should Know

COMMON SENSE dictates much of Chihuahua care. The breed requires the usual routines as used with other breeds, only in a much smaller proportion. There are a few things, however, which require a little more caution.

As previously mentioned, the Chihuahua has the molera, sometimes called the "fontanel," or soft spot on top of the skull. It is unique to the breed and is not considered a defect. The molera is very prominent in puppies, getting somewhat smaller as the puppy matures. Occasionally it will completely disappear. Do not be concerned if the molera remains, just practice a little more caution so head injuries do not occur, and be aware that if the molera is unusually large, there may be a health problem.

Caution should also be taken when picking up and holding the Chihuahua. The Chihuahua should be picked up with two hands, one under the body and one at the rear end, or under the loin. He must be held securely and close to the human body. Small dogs do not like to be held out in the air or left dangling. They want to feel some kind of security. The palm of one hand, after picking puppy up, should be under the chest of the dog. Do not let fingers rest between the dog's body and elbow. This will lead to elbows sticking

Holding the puppy correctly and securely will build confidence.

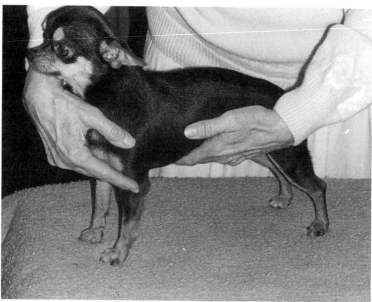

Ideally, the Chihuahua should be picked up with two hands, one under the body and the other under the loin.

out. Do not squeeze front legs together. This will lead to deformity of both legs and shoulders. The thumb and little finger should rest gently on the opposite sides of the dog, with the three middle fingers on the chest.

COMMON FAULTS AND PROBLEMS

Every breed of dog has some common physical faults, usually brought on by Man. Many of these faults will not alter the life span of the dog, and a pet with these faults may live to a very ripe old age. However, if these faults appear in potential breeding stock, these dogs should not be bred. They should be castrated or spayed and sold to loving homes as pet companions. The only way to breed out a fault is to use stock that does not have it.

Subluxation of the patella exists in many breeds. This is when the knee cap, or patella, does not slide smoothly in the trochlear groove. The lips or ridges surrounding the groove are not developed enough, or the groove is not deep enough to carry the movement of the patella. Surgery can alleviate a serious case, but with mild cases, the dog gets along very well, requires no surgery and leads quite a normal life. As the dog gets older, however, arthritis may set in.

Occasionally a puppy is born with a **cleft palate**. This is more common in the brachycephalic, or short-muzzle, round-skull breeds. In simplest terms, it is a defect involving a hole in the roof of the mouth. Dogs with this condition are unable to eat properly and usually have to be euthanized.

There is an occasional **heart murmur** problem. A puppy usually can live a full and happy life, just as humans with a heart murmur do. However, these dogs should not be used for breeding, only as pets.

Overshot or undershot mouths sometimes occur when muzzles are too long or too short. This is one of the most difficult things to breed out, and it sometimes takes a few generations of breeding to get rid of the problem. These dogs make perfectly good pets, although they should definitely not be used for breeding.

Hypoglycemia is a case of low blood sugar. It is occasionally seen in early puppyhood, and frequently the puppy outgrows this condition. It manifests itself with seizures, rigidity or limpness, poor mobility and sometimes unconsciousness. It may last for a few seconds or for several minutes. Puppy should be kept warm and fed

131

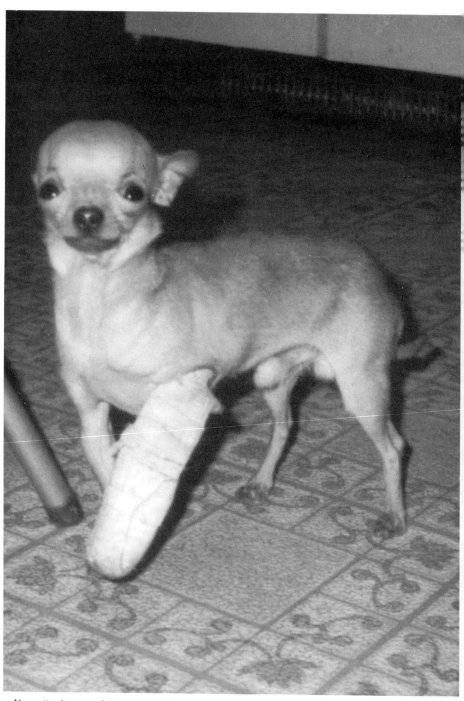

No matter how careful we are, accidents do happen. Here is Will O'Wisp Lil Bucky Buck'roo, owned by Millie Williams. A full recovery was in the future.

some kind of sugar, such as syrup or sugar mixed with water. Administer the sugar mixture slowly and carefully, so the puppy does not choke. Seek immediate veterinary help.

Hydrocephalus is excessive fluid in the cranium, manifesting itself in an unusually large head for the size of the dog. There is sometimes "east-west" eye placement, impairment of mobility, falling down frequently or just unsteadiness on legs. Most puppies do not live long with this condition, and euthanasia is recommended.

Death from anesthesia is not a truly common experience, but it occurs enough for breeders of small dogs to become very wary of the use of anesthesia for anything but the most necessary circumstances.

Ears that will not be erect are not noticeable in most Chihuahua puppies until after eight to ten weeks of age. During the teething stage, which can last a few months, the ears may go up and down. They may also go up and down several times during one day. If, however, the ears do not become erect at all by the time a puppy is ten weeks of age, it is time to help the ears to stand erect.

Taping the ears can be helpful, but this requires considerable care to prevent injury or permanent damage. One method is to take one paper match per ear and remove the flammable head of the match. Round the four corners of the paper match with an emery board to get rid of sharp edges. Clean the inner ear, then place the prepared match, center wise, over the fold. Tape the match on to the inner visible ear with "breathable" adhesive tape or "new skin" tape. With the match taped in place, put your forefinger behind the ear and bend the match and ear over the forefinger with your thumb. This will make the ear tip curl backwards, assisting it in becoming erect.

The tape and match should be removed every three days to let air circulate in the ear for a few hours, then retape. Treatment may take several weeks, enough time for the ear to grow strong.

Some breeders have used cod-liver oil tablets along with taping, the dosage adjusted for the weight of the puppy. Others use a vitamin/mineral/calcium supplement.

Before taping the ear of the Long Coat Chihuahua, the ears should be free of hair on the inside and the outside, to avoid carrying excess weight. Be very careful of the edges of the ears, which are thin and can be easily cut.

Ch. Okatoma Herron's I've Got Class with three-day-old pups. Owned by the Lamberts, Okatoma Kennels.

13

Breeding and Whelping the Chihuahua

BEFORE PREPARATIONS and arrangements for breeding a litter begin, let it be said that no breeding should take place with anything but the best possible quality Chihuahuas, both sire and dam. Of course, every dog will have some fault or two, but one must take care to breed only those animals with the least minor faults. Some faults are very difficult to overcome, and it takes several generations of breeding to purge the line of the fault. Other faults can be overcome in a generation or two. It is much easier to breed quality animals when starting with the best than it is to try to breed out glaring faults generation after generation.

If you are not certain if you have a quality, breedable bitch, discuss it with her breeder. If that breeder is not available, get opinions from at least three other knowledgeable people.

In addition to starting a breeding program with high-quality Chihuahuas, equally important is the maintenance of the breeding stock as well as the resultant litter. Maintenance involves medical care, physical care and mental care, including a happy relationship with human beings. Of course, the relationship with human beings is from birth throughout the Chihuahua's entire life.

All stock, breeding and companion dogs, must be fit and well maintained. It is the obligation of the breeder to see that a puppy goes to the right home, where mental and physical fitness will be provided for the life of the Chihuahua. Over the years of your breeding experience, you will encounter many new ways to improve upon whelping techniques and care of dam and puppies, as well as how to deal with the various problems that may occur.

Keep detailed, accurate records of everything. You should have records on the stud dog, brood bitch and puppies. The latter should include weighing, so you get an idea about the maturing process. For example, with most Chihuahua puppies, it takes ten to fourteen days to double their birth weight. At the end of the month, they have approximately quadrupled the birth weight. Whatever they weigh at three months, they double that weight at full maturity, within half a pound, either plus or minus.

Before deciding on breeding, you must decide whether to line breed, inbreed, or outcross.

With **inbreeding**, matings are based on very closely related animals: father to daughter, son to mother, brother to sister. This is supposed to correct physical and mental characteristics. There is always the danger, however, of bringing out the worst traits, in addition to the good qualities.

Outcrossing is directly opposite of inbreeding. This is the breeding of absolutely unrelated dogs within a specific breed.

Linebreeding is between inbreeding and outcrossing. It is the mating of animals that are only distantly related, such as uncles to nieces, nephews to aunts, cousins to cousins.

If you are inexperienced, linebreeding is suggested as the best way to go. Inbreeding should be used only by the most experienced breeder. Outcrossing, if used judiciously, can be very beneficial to your breeding program, when you have gained some experience.

Before breeding, be certain that you have a clear understanding with your veterinarian that you may call him/her at any time of day or night and that you will get an immediate response, not a wait-and-see attitude. If your veterinarian is not willing to perform a Caesarian section at two or three o'clock in the morning, you had better seek the services of another.

SELECTING A STUD DOG

When selecting a stud dog, if you have your own male, do not use him at too young an age. Try him at about nine to ten months and then about every six weeks until about fifteen months old. Overuse of a young stud dog can physically ruin him, and excessive use of a stud dog has been known to cause early death. In the early breeding programs of beginners, it is better to seek service from experienced studs than to maintain your own stud dog.

The sire you select must be of good type, both physically and mentally sound. He must have been well cared for. If the bitch has never had a litter, it is better to obtain stud service from an experienced stud dog.

Seek a stud dog that has the qualities you most admire. Try to locate offspring from the sire you are contemplating. Some offspring will be good, some not so good and some will be average.

Remember that 50 percent of the genes will come from the sire dog and 50 percent from the dam. It is ridiculous to blame only the stud dog for the quality of the litter if it is poor, and just as silly to give full credit to the stud dog for a high-quality litter. You will not find a perfect dog, so do not look for one. Look for a stud dog from a positive viewpoint, not a negative one. Seek a stud with major positive virtues, but do not discard him as a possibility because he has a minor fault or two. And do not turn down a superb stud dog because you do not like his owner.

Both prospective sire and dam should be in good health. An examination by the veterinarian is in order for both. At the very least, a brucellosis test should be given.

Brucellosis in bitches can lead to failure to conceive or aborting of puppies. Infection in males can be transferred to the bitches. Males infected with brucellosis may have enlargement of the genitalia or atrophy of same. The lymph nodes may be enlarged and the sperm count may be low.

Bitches should not be bred at their first season, which occurs anytime after six months of age. Some bitches do not come into season until closer to a year, or even eighteen months of age. It is best to wait until the bitch is at least one year old and into her second season, as a minimum. If the bitch is a late bloomer, it is still wise to wait another season before breeding.

Do not wait until the bitch is four years old to breed her. That is much too old to breed for the first time. Neither should she be bred every heat period, and definitely not after she is eight years old. Breeding every other season as a maximum is considered safe for the bitch.

SIGNING A CONTRACT

Once you have decided upon the stud dog, the next step is to have a contract prepared, defining agreement between owner(s) of the stud dog and owner(s) of the bitch to be bred. The bare minimum facts to be included in the contract are identification of stud dog and bitch, including all AKC registration numbers and stud book numbers, if available. Keep in mind that both sire and dam must be registered with the AKC in order to register the litter. The contract should also include addresses and telephone numbers of all owners. Mention the date(s) of mating and when litter is due. Include conditions of the breeding such as fee, when the fee is to be paid, or possible pick or second choice of litter in lieu of fee. It is recommended to pay the stud fee, for there may be only one puppy in the litter. If you have opted to give pick of the litter to the stud dog owner, you may end up having a bitch with a Caesarian section, shipping fees and all the other expenses and aggravation, with no puppy for you. It is also possible that the entire litter may not survive. The contract should state that you are entitled to one other stud service, at no further charge, if there is no conception, or if puppies do not survive after X number of days. Fourteen days is considered a reasonable amount of time to determine puppy survival. The next replacement stud service may have to be from another dog, as the first one may not be available.

Written agreements lead to continued good relationships between parties. Oral agreements lead to misunderstandings and hurt feelings, and can destroy what was once a good friendship. At all times, treat each other in a fair and honest manner.

THE BREEDING

The first noticeable sign that a bitch is coming into season is the enlargement of the vulva at the entrance to the vagina. Even at this stage, a male may show interest, although the bitch will not. Sometimes during this early stage of oestrus (reproductive cycle) the bitch will urinate more often. She may even go off her feed for a day or two.

The next stage to look for is a red discharge. This stage is of the utmost importance. Mark it on your calendar. For the next several days, keep a close watch. The red will become more pink, gradually becoming straw-color or colorless over the next few days. This is the time when your bitch will be ready to breed, usually within ten to fourteen days after the first red discharge. Desire in the stud dog will be strong, and your bitch will stand upright for the male, curling her tail over to one side. Although the ten to fourteen days from first showing of color is the normal conception time, this has been known to vary considerably, so it is essential that accurate records be kept of each mating.

It will be easier to mate the dog and bitch if two people are present to assist. Mating may be achieved easier if you let the stud and the bitch engage in a little love-dance play before getting down to serious business. This is good practice for the average dog, one who is not overly aggressive. He will be slower and take his time. If the bitch is too aggressive, she will have to be held firmly, or she may scare the dog away.

If the angle of the vagina is steep, it will be easier for the dog to penetrate. The longer the vagina, the easier to obtain a "tie," wherein the stud dog becomes temporarily joined to the bitch by an enlarged bulb of erectile tissue.

This tie, or locking together, may last only a few seconds, or it could last over an hour. An average tie is ten to twenty minutes. With two people present, one to hold the bitch and one to hold the stud, there is less likelihood of any injury to dog or bitch occurring during the mating. Also, if either stud or bitch has to be repositioned, two people assisting can make it simpler. Sometimes a stud dog wants to turn around or get off the bitch and turn completely in the opposite direction. This requires human assistance, or injury can occur to one or both animals.

Mating should take place in a room where there are no distractions. This is especially necessary with inexperienced Chihuahuas. Use a high table, covered with a nonslip material and barriers around the edge, so the animals cannot fall off. An alternate method is for two people to sit on the floor facing each other, with human legs as a barrier to keep animals within a confined space. Sometimes a dog is too short for the bitch, so his rear legs may have to be elevated with some sort of padding.

Both dog and bitch should be well rested before mating, and they should not be mated just after eating. Many breeders prefer to mate the pair twice, skipping a day in between. Others prefer only one mating, believing that the puppies will be more uniform in size than when mating is spread over three or four days.

Some studs are very aggressive, in which case the bitch will need a calming influence by being talked to and petted, so she does not become frightened.

If the bitch was shipped in for service from your stud dog, it is better to wait a few days after the mating before returning her. Make all the arrangements and ask the owner to call you upon the bitch's arrival home, as you should have done when she arrived at your location.

The gestation period is about sixty-three days. This may vary a day or two. If puppies are born before fifty-eight days, the chance of survival is very poor. If the bitch carries three days over her delivery date and you have counted the days of gestation correctly, there is cause for concern. A Caesarian section is probably in order, otherwise both dam and litter may die.

During gestation, food intake should be increased. Discuss the advisability of vitamin and mineral supplements with your veterinarian before adding them to the bitch's diet. Some breeders prefer the addition of raspberry leaves to the diet, claiming that this makes for easier whelping and less chance of the need to have a Caesarian section. There has been no scientific research done in this area, but there are many breeders who are willing to swear that they have had positive results with natural whelping through the use of raspberry leaves.

Continue to exercise the bitch, but do not overdo it. Try shorter walks and unstressful play. Avoid unnecessary medications and X-rays, especially during the early and mid-weeks of gestation. If an X-ray is required to determine size of a single pup and the possibility of a Caesarian, this should be done no more than four days before the due date.

THE WHELPING

Caesarian sections are not uncommon, as some Chihuahuas are not natural whelpers. Caesarian sections must be repeated if a bitch has a small pelvis and does not dilate during labor. Limit Caesarian sections, then have the bitch spayed.

About two weeks before puppies are due, prepare a quiet place with a whelping box. This will give the bitch time to get acquainted with what will be her new surroundings for a few weeks.

A day or so before whelping time, the bitch's temperature will

The puppy is completely out and ready to be cleaned. If the dam is slow, it is better to assist her by removing the sac, then cutting the cord and drying the puppy.   *Terry*

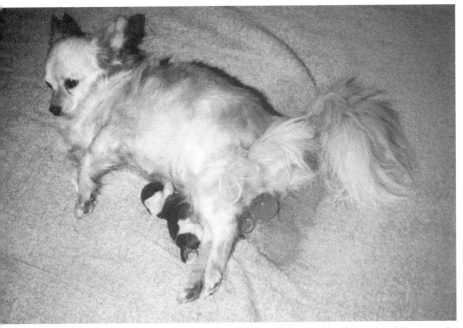

The first puppy begins to nurse while the water bag emerges in preparation for arrival of the second puppy. The nursing puppy can now be put on a heating pad so the dam can concentrate on the arrival of the next puppy.   *Terry*

141

begin to drop. A few hours before, the temperature may go as low as 97 degrees. This is a good sign that whelping time is very near. The bitch may become quieter, alternating with digging in her whelping box. She will vigorously rip at the papers with her teeth. She will pant heavily and make crying sounds. Usually, she will not eat, although it has been known that some bitches eat right up to whelping time. In that case, they may regurgitate.

As the vulva becomes softer, there will be a colorless, or pale straw color discharge. Then she will go into hard labor of straining or pushing motions, raising her head with each push. She may also cry louder, especially if this is a new experience for her. Keep a time check between each hard push or heavy labor. This stage should not go beyond three hours maximum without whelping a puppy. Some breeders allow only two hours, but if the bitch is not screaming and there is no green discharge, a little longer wait before seeking veterinary assistance is usually all right. First-time whelpers sometimes take a little longer to deliver the first puppy.

Before the first puppy arrives, there will be an emergence of a "water bag." Novice breeders sometimes mistake this for a puppy. The purpose of the water bag is to ease the passage of the forthcoming puppy, by enlarging the birth passage. A puppy usually follows soon after the water bag. A green discharge before a puppy is born indicates separation of umbilical cord from the unborn puppy, which may be dead.

When the puppy is halfway out, and if you wish to assist, hold the partly emerged puppy and pull downward gently only when the bitch pushes. Otherwise, you may break the sac in which the puppy is encased, thereby causing the puppy to drown in the fluid. If the emerging puppy is slippery, hold on to it with a soft paper towel or cloth. Assist in delivery only if the bitch needs help in expelling the puppy, or whelp, as it is sometimes called.

With the birth of the puppy encased in the sac, the umbilical cord will be attached to the puppy at one end and to the placenta, or afterbirth, at the other end. The placenta is still providing oxygen and nourishment to the puppy at this stage. Do not cut the cord until you have cleared the sac away from the entire head of the puppy, so it can breathe on its own when the cord is cut. Clamp the cord with a sterile surgical clamp, then cut the cord about one and one-half inches from the puppy's abdomen. Let the clamp remain on this small section of the cord for a couple of minutes to prevent loss of blood. Another method is to tie the umbilical cord with sterile string and then cut, keeping the string on to prevent bleeding.

If you do not assist the dam, she will rip away the sac with her teeth, so the puppy can breathe. She will sever the umbilical cord and then eat the placenta. Watch carefully, that in severing the cord the dam does not get too close to puppy's abdomen, for she could accidentally tear it open. Eating the placenta has been said to help provide quick nourishment for the dam and stimulate milk production. Too many placentas eaten can also cause diarrhea. Whether or not you allow the dam to eat some or none of the placentas is the breeder's choice. The author's preference is to dispose of all placentas immediately. Make certain to account for one placenta for each puppy. If a placenta is retained within the dam, infection could result.

If you are assisting the dam in cleaning puppies, try this method. After removing the entire sac and the cord has been tied and cut, hold the puppy with its head in a downward position and shake gently but firmly to expel liquid from the mouth and lungs. At the same time rub the puppy dry with a firm motion using warm, dry towels. This is similar to the dam licking the puppy dry. You will soon hear the first squeak from the puppy. When it is dry, gently rub around the anus to expel the waxlike substance from the rectum. Now clean and dry, the pup can be placed at the dam's nipple for its first meal. Hold each pup there until it shows a strong sucking motion.

Place clean, dry papers in with the dam for the arrival of the next puppy. When labor begins for the next arrival, place the last puppy in a previously prepared box that has a heating pad turned on low. The heating pad should be covered with soft, nonsnagging material. Do not use indoor-outdoor carpeting. Puppy urine combined with carpet chemicals will burn the puppy's skin. Keep checking that the pad is not too hot. Heat can kill, as can chilling.

When all puppies have arrived, clean the whelping box once again, put in all fresh material and replace all the puppies. Do not keep the room too hot, the dam will become uncomfortable. Seventy-two degrees, with the puppies and dam out of all drafts, is sufficient. The whelping box should be large enough so that a heating pad covered with nonsnag toweling is at one end and clean papers at the other end. This way, the dam or the puppies can get to a cooler spot if necessary. The whelping box sides should be too high for puppies to fall out, but low enough so the dam can jump out.

For the first two weeks, the whelping box should be by your bedside. You will not get much sleep, but you will get a litter of live, healthy puppies, if a careful watch has been kept.

After a little rest, some light nourishment is in order for Ch. Marsubri's Tia Ruff, C.D. *Terry*

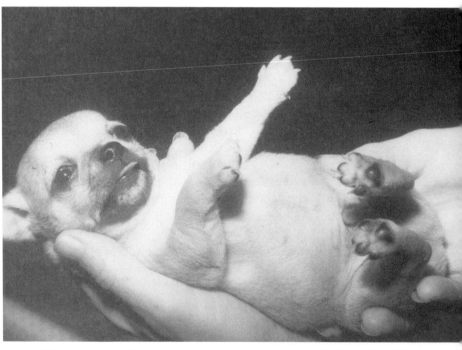

This is a lovely, healthy, plump puppy, four weeks old, owned by Brooke Kaye-Albright.

144

This description is of a normal birth. If complications should occur, do not delay. Consult your veterinarian immediately. Delay can mean death for puppies and/or dam.

With each successive litter, you will gain more experience. Keep a detailed log of each whelping. Weigh puppies every day for the first month, then weekly thereafter, and every month from three months to maturity. This will keep you informed about the amount of nourishment they are getting, as well as learning growth patterns of Chihuahua puppies and in particular lines. Puppies may vary in size. It is a good idea to have a scale that measures in quarter ounces. A Chihuahua puppy should gain at least one quarter ounce per day for the first week, in order to survive.

Puppies will vary in size at birth. The average size of a Chihuahua puppy will be around three to three and a half ounces at birth. The size of puppies may be determined by how many times the bitch was bred and at what period she actually conceived.

FEEDING

Tube feeding is a practical way of providing nourishment for newborns that are too weak to nurse normally or for orphaned puppies. It has one great disadvantage in that it does not instill the sucking motion that newborns need. But, if done properly, tube feeding is cleaner, quicker and hassle free.

French tube #5, or smaller, that is used for premature infants, works fine with Chihuahua puppies. The tubes are individually packaged and presterilized. The tube, along with a syringe, and formula are all that is needed. The formula may be a commercially prepared liquid; there are three or four of these on the market.

Begin by measuring the tube, laying it from the front of the puppy's mouth down the neck and chest, past the sternum, to about the end of the ribcage, or just above the navel. This is the stomach location. Make a permanent mark with tape or ink on the tube. This ensures that you do not put too much tube into the puppy's stomach. Connect tube to syringe and bring the warm, not hot, formula to within one-eighth inch of the end of the tube to expel all the air. Hold the puppy in a semi-upright or upright position with one hand. With the other hand, gently slide the tube down the middle of the puppy's throat. The puppy will draw the tube inward with its tongue. If you have to push the tube, or it will not slide down the throat easily, you

Babies are hard work, says Ch. Okatoma's Little Bita Whiskey, with six-week-old pups Buck and Peeper. Both puppies completed championships and are owned by the Lamberts.

Merryway's Sepia with an exceptionally large litter of six, about four days old. Owner, Susan F. Payne.

are not in the esophagus. Remove the tube and start again. Slide the tube all the way into the puppy until you reach the permanent mark you have made on the tube. This means you have reached the stomach.

Very slowly depress the syringe. "Slowly" is the key word here. You want to try to simulate the speed at which a puppy eats. If you try to feed quickly, the stomach will distend too rapidly and the puppy may regurgitate. Some formula may come out the nose or even get into the lungs. If the abdomen becomes too distended before the formula has been completely put into the stomach, do not continue feeding. Remove the tube immediately. Do this carefully, so the formula does not continue to flow while the tube is being withdrawn from the puppy.

Caution: Be sure to check the formula's temperature before giving it to the puppy. It should neither be ice cold nor hot. Test it on your wrist before using.

The amount to feed a three-ounce puppy will be about 1½ to 2 cc of formula, every two hours around the clock. Some puppies will take more per feeding, others less. You will be able to tell how much a puppy needs by the roundness of the abdomen.

Clean the tube and the syringe immediately upon completion of feeding. These are cleaned by filling the syringe with boiled water and pressing the syringe plunger to shoot water through the tube until both are clean. This must be done as soon as feeding is complete so formula does not stick to the inside of the tube.

Go back to the puppy and gently rub along its back and around the genital organs and anus to simulate the dam's cleaning with her tongue. This will stimulate the puppy to urinate and defecate. Rubbing the back will help to expel any air that may have inadvertently gotten into the stomach.

When this has been accomplished, cuddle the puppy and stroke gently. Talk or make cooing sounds. This will introduce loving care and human handling, which in turn will be the beginning of training for both the show ring and home companionship. This kind of upbringing makes for a mentally stable and happy dog.

Bottle feeding is another alternative. The only advantage it has over tube feeding is that it provides the natural sucking mechanism for the puppy. There are premature human infant nipples available, as well as tiny nursing bottles. The nipple holes should be of a size to enable a weak puppy to extract formula easily, but not so fast that he chokes. Test formula for correct temperature before using. This

Sable, a German Shepherd owned by Susan Payne, is helping to raise a large litter of Chihuahuas. Not all dogs are suitable as foster mothers, but Sable is doing an excellent job.

A six-week-old Chihuahua pup called April, owned by Susan Payne, and the German Shepherd, Teddy, became good friends.

bottle feeding method takes a longer time, but it is closest to natural feeding and the puppy gets a lot of cuddling at the same time. Stimulation of puppy as noted above remains the same.

During your lifetime of breeding you will face disappointment at the results of a litter, see puppies dying for no apparent reason, maybe lose a dam under anesthesia, and lose your older dogs. But over the years you will find yourself becoming a dedicated breeder, through the good times and the bad, because you love Chihuahuas so much. Your love for the breed will keep you going and there will be many happy memories that these dogs and puppies will give to you.

Chihuahuas can be taught tricks very easily. Here is Ch. Eric's Joe Louie Chip of Oz, having just won Best Veteran at the CC of Mid-Jersey, 1988.

14

The Character of the Chihuahua

ALTHOUGH IT IS diminutive in size, there is nothing diminutive about the character of the Chihuahua. Precisely because of the size, they are good pets and companions, and yes, they can be utilized in some specific working programs.

Chihuahuas adjust easily to new surroundings and climates and quickly become devoted to all members of the household, with evidence of love and trust toward those who handle them gently. As the breed is very people oriented, they are quite attentive and thus easily trained. This is reinforced by their innate intelligence and good memory.

Chihuahuas are spirited little dogs and like to play with each other as well as with the family members. Early socialization is as important in this breed as in any other. They will become shy only if the owners fail to provide early socialization with humans outside the family. Any dog will develop a wary attitude toward outsiders if they become completely sheltered house pets. To avoid shyness in any breed, it is essential that outside socialization begin at a very early stage in the animal's life, preferably by the time it is two to three months of age. Most breeders will take care of this so that puppies will easily adjust to new environments at any age.

Best friends are Blue Sky's Cheri O' Wildwood and Concord's Hallmark, dogs owned by Kathy and Mark Lenhart.

Summer fun is enjoyed by Rudy; Jeffery Pierre; Fonzie, CDX; Ch. Skeeter, CDX; Joey; Bo, CDX (a Dachsy friend); and Buster. These dogs are owned by the Lamberts, Okatoma Kennels. Dogs must be very well trained to be able to participate in boating activities.

Ch. Okatoma's Blaze Away Gremlin, also known as Gizmo, getting ready for a belly rub. Owned by the Lamberts.

Ch. Terrymont Trifle Bit of Candy, CDX, as a very young puppy. Chihuahuas like to have a warm and draft-free place to nap.

If a Chihuahua becomes shy or vicious, the problem can be laid right at the owner's doorstep. With dog ownership comes responsibility. Early outside socialization is part of the owner's responsibility.

Size is not a prerequisite to becoming a good watchdog. Chihuahuas have rather acute hearing and sight senses, thus making outstanding guardians. They can differentiate between the owner's and a stranger's footfall, and can recognize the sound of a different car engine entering the driveway.

Because the Chihuahua prefers human companionship, once a Chihuahua owner, always a Chihuahua owner. They are captivating little dogs, and quickly make a place for themselves in your heart and soul.

15

How to Show
a Chihuahua

AS IN MOST kinds of training, whether it be for conformation, obedience or well-behaved house dogs, there are usually basic handling techniques that are suitable for all breeds and all sizes of dogs. Once these are learned, the next step is the handling that is suited for your particular breed and need. From there, we continue with techniques that are for a particular dog within a breed. In other words, even though there are basic handling techniques, these must be adapted to each individual dog within a breed.

It is not proper to make a generalized statement that "This is how to show a Chihuahua." Yes, there are general techniques applicable to the breed, but we must remember that you are dealing with individual dogs, hence there will be techniques that are used for some Chihuahuas and not others. It is possible to pick up handling know-how just by watching professionals in many other breeds. Some techniques can be used for the Chihuahua, others cannot. Only by watching other people and other breeds, discussions with professional handlers or breeders, and by actually practicing at matches or training schools, will you learn how to handle your dog. Much of good handling is simple common sense. After discussions with others and observations of handling techniques, pick and choose what is

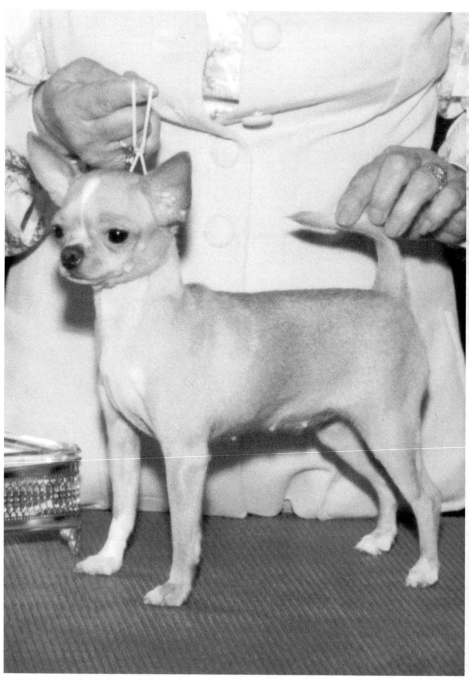

Ch. Call's Delightful Design, in limited showing, had six Bests in Show and many Bests in Specialty. She was the top Smooth Coat 1981–82 and top Chihuahua. She was selected as the ideal Smooth Coat Chihuahua by the Chihuahua Club of America. Owners, Annie D. and Chester P. Call. *Cott/Francis*

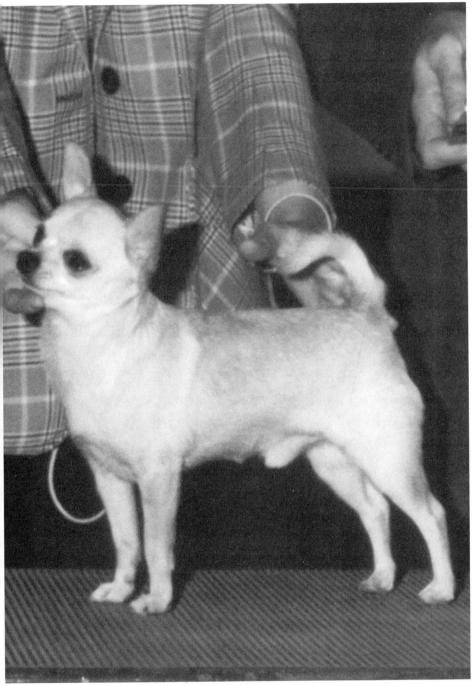

Ch. Ouachitah For Your Eyes Only, a Best in Show winner and the first Chihuahua to win the Toy Group at Westminster KC, February 1984. Breeder/owner, Linda George. *Alverson*

Ch. GinJim's Royal Acres Mervyn. Although shown on a limited scale, he had eight Group Firsts, forty other Group placings and seven Specialty Bests of Breed. He was the Number 1 Long Coat from 1979 through 1982. Breeder, Joyce E. Flint; owner, Virginia W. Smith. *Callea*

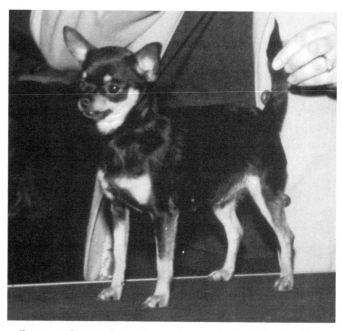

Terrymont Smooth Samantha, on her way to her championship at Westminster KC. Breeder/owner, E. Ruth Terry, Terrymont Kennels. *Gilbert*

applicable for your particular dog. Discard some suggestions and retain others.

Training begins early. In fact, one could say it begins from the first day of life because the touching, cuddling and talking is the beginning of puppy/human relationship. It is the beginning training for puppy to acquire confidence in himself and in others. Although we rely on producing puppies with good genes, we must also remember that an extremely large contribution toward proper puppy behavior is achieved through the everyday environmental experience. Thus, early training in socialization, confidence and proper behavior in the Chihuahua is vitally important.

When the puppy is about five weeks of age, put a narrow, lightweight collar on it. Use a buckle-type or Velcro-attachment closing, not a choke training collar. Puppy will get used to this neck adornment, will stop scratching at it in a few days, and will be less likely to fight the lead later on.

Puppy will be ready for lead breaking at about six weeks of age. The sessions must be enjoyable for both puppy and trainer. Do not train when you are angry or tired, as it may lead to a confrontation with the recalcitrant puppy. Sessions are to be kept short and accompanied with happy tones of voice. At first, let puppy go wherever he wishes, then gradually make the leash more taut and start guiding the puppy around.

He will feel more confident if the training sessions take place in familiar territory, such as a long hallway in the house, out of doors in the backyard, or in the driveway. If the driveway is made of black hardtop, do not train there on a hot, sunny day, as the asphalt will get extremely hot and may burn the pads of the puppy's feet.

Puppies learn quickly at this age. In a few short sessions, you will find that the puppy is going just where you are guiding him with the lead. When the puppy is doing well in familiar territory, it is then time to go elsewhere for a lesson. This may be a local park, school grounds, or outside a shopping mall. Be sure to check about the local dog ordinances if you are going to public areas.

TABLE TRAINING

Stacking, also known as posing, is best learned on a nonskid table top. The table must be steady. With show lead on the puppy, place the other end over your shoulder. With the left hand, place

Ch. Regalaire's Masked Marvel, JR. Has five Best in Specialty wins with twenty-four Group placings for breeder/owners Joseph and Mozelle Smith. Here he demonstrates proper table stance.

Ch. Genbrook Pittore China Doll, shown by breeder/owner Brooke Kaye-Albright, illustrates one of the rewards of early table training.

forefinger along the flank, with a slight pressure. This will prevent the puppy from sitting down. With the right hand, begin stroking your puppy, beginning at the brisket, ending under the chin and bringing palm forward in front of the puppy's face. At the same time, talk in a soothing tone of voice and pronounce a word such as "stand," "pose," or "show."

When he has learned the table pose, you will find it much easier to transfer to floor training. If he has learned the table lesson well, all that will be necessary is for you to use your right hand, and say the word you have chosen, such as "stand." The well-trained puppy will go into a show pose with no stacking effort on your part, even on the floor.

The table training can be used equally well for both breed and obedience. Table training first makes it much easier on the trainer and instills confidence in the puppy.

When on the table, some Chihuahuas have a tendency to lift one front foot. No amount of pulling or tugging the leg downward will help to bring it down. To make the leg and foot go back into position, locate the highest points of the withers with thumb and forefinger. Using either thumb or forefinger, put pressure on the top of the withers on the side the leg is raised. The leg will go down immediately and will stay down.

Baiting is a matter of handler preference. Some dogs pose better using bait. The bait can be food or a toy. For unresponsive males, it is possible to perk the dog up by using a handkerchief covered with a female's "in-season" scent. Other Chihuahuas bait equally well with voice tones, or with the rattling of noisy, crinkly paper. Each Chihuahua is an individual and will require training for that particular dog.

Gaiting is to be done at the correct speed for the individual dog. Have someone gait the dog for you, coming toward you, going away from you and in a large circular pattern. If the dog moves too closely, slow down. Do not confuse closeness, a fault, with the natural convergence toward a center line as speed increases. It may be necessary to use one speed going away and another speed coming back to the judge.

If you do not have anyone who can assist you in determining the correct gaiting speed, an alternative is to place a mirror at the end of a long hall and move toward it. However, this will only give you an idea about forward motion unless you cover the entire area with mirrors.

Ch. Stober's Monty Wooly was bred by the renowned Long Coat breeder
Anne Stober and owned by Terrymont Kennels, Herbert and E. Ruth Terry.
His handler, Barbara Partridge, gaited him to his championship.

Ashbey

Ch. Hurd's Sorceress Sue, gaited to the title for breeder/owner
Max Hurd, handled by Linda George.   *Kullander*

The best method of determining the proper gaiting speed and other handling techniques for you and your Chihuahua is to use the electronic marvel of our times, the VCR. With this method of observing and evaluating your handling and training capabilities, you will have a permanent record of your work and can use the techniques many years later with other dogs.

Chihuahuas should be gaited and shown on a loose lead. Tight leads indicate either poorly trained dogs, poorly constructed dogs or a lack of trainer confidence in the dog's qualities. A dog cannot gait properly with a tight lead.

GAITING PATTERNS

Knowing the most basic ring patterns and how to execute them will build your confidence and skill in showing your Chihuahua to its full potential.

The most common gaiting patterns include a counterclockwise circle both individually and with the entire class. The **triangle,** with the first leg straight out, the second leg turning to the left across the ring, and the third leg going back to the judge, may be the most popular pattern. If you have trouble gaiting the dog in a straight line, focus your eyes on something ahead of you, such as a tree or someone wearing a bright article of clothing. This will keep you going in the right direction.

Down and back, also called up and down, is a straight line away from the judge and a straight line back to the judge.

The **T pattern** is only used occasionally, as it is too time consuming. With the T pattern, the dog is gaited down the center of the ring, turns either right or left toward the outer side of the ring, turns and goes across the full width of the ring, back to the midline of the ring to return to the judge.

With all patterns, upon returning to the judge, have your dog stand or pose with a voice and/or hand signal.

JUDGING

No matter how well your Chihuahua is trained and no matter how outstanding the quality, you will not win if your dog is in poor physical condition or poorly groomed. A winning dog must be free of disease and any parasites and groomed to perfection.

Ch. H and J's Mystic Wizard won the Toy Group with Linda George, handler, for owners Jack Phariss and Linda George. Breeder, Jack Phariss. *Booth*

Ch. KC's Cujo of Blue Skys was shown by owner Kathy Lenhart. Cujo has won several Specialty shows and numerous Group placements. Breeder, Peggy L. Bailey. *Graham*

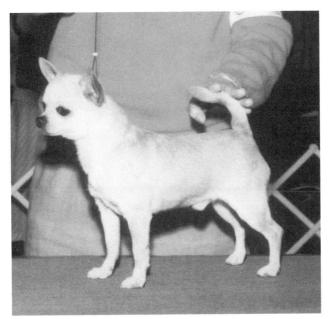

Ch. Desmond's Merry Maker, Best in Specialty and Group winner.
Owner, Lorie F. Gibbs. *Sosa*

Ch. Dartan Pirate Swashbuckler. Owner, Darwin Delaney; co-owner,
Tanya Delaney. *Booth*

Ch. Ouachitah Beau Chiene, Best of Variety at the CCA, October 1988. One of only four Long Coats in American history to go Best in Show at an all-breed event. Breeder, Linda George; owner, Nancy Shapland.

During this time of breeding and training your dogs for the show ring, it is important to keep in mind on what points your dogs will be judged.

First will come judgment of **type.** Type may vary somewhat, depending on the lines from which it is descended. All breeds will have some variations within good specimens of the breed. Just how wide a variation is allowed will be determined by the Standard and the person doing the judging that day. Important breed traits and characteristics will also be assessed.

The **balance** of the dog will be taken into consideration. All the parts should fit together in correct proportion to all the other parts. This will be determined from both posing and gaiting.

The **soundness** of the dog is assessed in two parts: physical and mental. The physical soundness will show up in gaiting; the mental soundness will be apparent in demeanor, the dog's reaction to the judge's examination as well as to other dogs and people in the ring.

In addition to the above, other characteristics to be assessed are proper **grooming** for the breed and the **charisma** of the exhibit.

Breeding and showing dogs brings with it great responsibility: the future of our breed, the provision of good homes for the puppies and the interaction of the breed with society.

Ch. Rose's Harmony Dina-Mite, handled by Tara Setmayer, age twelve, for owner Helen Rose. This team won Best of Opposite Sex at the 1988 Westminster KC show.

16

Junior Showmanship

THE CLASSES NOW known as Junior Showman-
ship began several decades ago and went through various name
changes along the way. Many of today's professional handlers began
their careers in the Junior Showmanship Classes. At one time these
classes were judged only by professional handlers; today they are
judged by regularly approved breed judges or by those who are
approved to judge Junior Showmanship Classes only.

Junior Showmanship Classes are to be considered a vital and
important part of the dog show scene. Assignments for these classes
must be taken seriously and judged with great care. The judge must
officiate with zeal and responsibility.

Showing dogs can be an immensely satisfying and enjoyable
family sport. While the experienced handler-parents are exhibiting
in the conformation ring, the children can begin to learn the techniques of handling and proper ring procedure by entering Junior
Showmanship competition.

While there are no minimum or maximum age limitations in
most of the dog exhibiting areas, as long as the person handling the
dog is capable of doing so, there are age limitations in the Junior
Showmanship Classes. The usual classes are broken down into four
divisions. Novice Junior is for boys and girls at least ten years old
and under fourteen years who have not won three firsts in competi-

Susan G. Terry, the author's daughter, at age ten showing Ch. Terrymont Peach Parfait.

Brian E. Terry, the author's son, at age thirteen handling Ch. Kay's Don La Rico-L.
Holiday

170

Ch. Pittore Pazzazita Picante, handled by
Judy Gurin at the Dallas Chihuahua Club,
for owner Patricia Pittore.

Daughter of Mark and Kathy Lenhart, Melissa Lenhart, is showing Blue Sky's Cheri
O' Wildwood to Best in Match.

tion in a Novice Class. Open Junior is for age ten and under fourteen years who have won three firsts in Novice with competition. Novice Senior is at least fourteen years old and under eighteen who have not won three firsts in competition in Novice Class. Open Senior is for age fourteen and under eighteen who have won three firsts in Novice with competition.

There may also be a Best Junior Handler competition for the winner of each of the regular Junior Classes, if undefeated at that show. Detailed regulations and guidelines for the Junior Showmanship Classes may be obtained from the AKC.

These classes are held so that youngsters can be introduced to the sport of dogs and learn to handle their dogs with skill and sportsmanship in competition with their peers. Here they become accustomed to both winning and losing with grace. The child should be aware of proper ring procedure, and have or learn to have the ability to show a dog with skill and finesse.

Judging is based solely on the ability of the youngster to handle and show the dog in a manner appropriate for that particular breed. In other words, the handling of a giant breed or a mid-size breed would be considerably different from the way a Chihuahua is handled. The quality of the dogs is not evaluated in Junior Showmanship Classes.

The basic evaluations recommended by the AKC for the judge to officiate are:

Proper breed presentation, skill in handling the individual dog, appearance, and conduct.

The junior should not be ostentatious in attire nor in handling the dog; neither should he or she fade into the background. The dog should be groomed appropriately for the breed and the junior should be groomed appropriately for being an exhibitor.

Every handler movement should be smooth, natural, and skillful, bringing out the best of the dog while moving and while posing. This is teamwork between human and animal. There should be rapport between handler and dog, an apparent loving bond between them. They should not work like automatons.

The junior must have the dog under control at all times and not interfere with any other dog or handler. All should display a spirit of sportsmanship and courtesy whether winning or losing.

172

17

The Chihuahua
in Obedience

DESPITE ITS relatively small size, the Chihuahua has achieved remarkable feats in what is thought of as a working-type environment. Specific areas are Obedience Trials and Tracking events.

In AKC Obedience Trials and Tracking Tests, Chihuahuas compete and compare favorably with other breeds. There are several levels of competition, each succeeding level more difficult than the previous one.

In the area of Obedience Trials, the Chihuahua readily sheds his image of being a lap dog. Although known as the smallest dog in the world, the Chihuahua is equal to many large breeds of dogs in the high performance expected in obedience, whether it is simple around-the-house proper behavior, or outstanding performance in the more highly specialized training for competition.

As breeders, we must strive to retain the best physical and mental qualities of our Chihuahuas so they are capable of performing in both conformation and obedience competition. Thus, they must have the qualities of good conformation type, so we easily recognize the dog as a good Chihuahua; at the same time, we need the charisma, the mental and physical soundness, and the intelligence bred

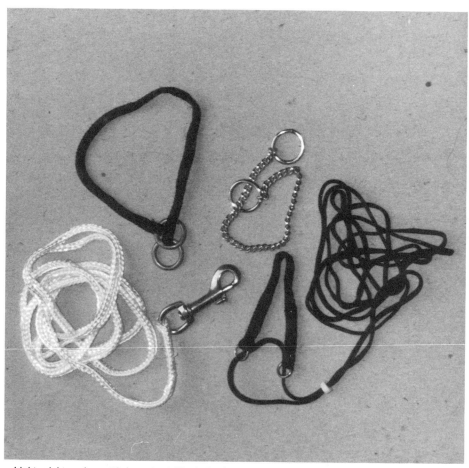

Lightweight equipment is important. Clockwise from upper left are a nylon training collar, a metal training collar, a martingale show lead and a nylon leash with a small snap attachment.

into the dogs so that they can be loving companions who are also capable of work in conformation and obedience competition.

As breeders we must not compartmentalize our dogs, saying this one is good for conformation showing, and this one is good for obedience competition. There is no reason that a Chihuahua cannot be an all-around dog; a loving companion, a conformation exhibit and a good obedience worker. This is the ultimate Chihuahua. Of course, there will be variations. Some will be better looking, while others will be quicker to learn a skill. With careful and thoughtful breeding, all these qualities can be maintained.

There has been many a Chihuahua that has achieved a conformation championship, obedience titles, and/or tracking titles. Chihuahuas can have beauty, intelligence, stamina, charisma and the characteristics needed for all aspects of exhibiting, all rolled into one package.

Quoting from the AKC manual, Obedience Regulations: "The purpose of Obedience Trials is to demonstrate the usefulness of the pure-bred dog as a companion of man," and "It is also essential that the dog demonstrate willingness and enjoyment of its work. . . ."

Obedience training requires an understanding of why your dog behaves or reacts in a certain manner. If you do not know at the beginning of training, you will most likely learn the whys and wherefores of behavioral response as training progresses. In other words, training your dog leads to understanding your dog, and understanding your dog will make you a better trainer. You will also gain coordination in working with an animal. This coordination will be useful in conformation training, as well.

Training for both conformation and obedience at the same time is quite possible. It depends on the level of intelligence and age of the dog. Many dogs are able to cope, merely by a change in equipment: show lead versus obedience lead and collar. Usually, no change in the type of commands used is needed.

In fact, while training for obedience one is inadvertently also training for conformation, although the trainer may not realize it. In both cases, the dog must be able to follow around on a lead, must be able to stand for examination, or pose, must be responsive to the handler, must obey commands. These are all things that are done in the Novice Obedience Class and beyond.

There are some things that may be considered obstacles for the Chihuahua in obedience. If handled correctly, they need not be obstacles at all.

Ch. Brite Star Galactic Firework, practicing the **heeling** exercise for his CD title. Owner, Elizabeth Bickel.

A lineup of Brite Star obedience Chihuahuas practicing the **Long Down**, an *Open* exercise. Left to right are Tasia, CDX; Apollo, CD; Orion, CD; Ch. Charlie Coco, CDX; Daisy; Ch. Chrissy, CD; Ch. Queenie. All are training for their next obedience titles. Owner, Elizabeth Bickel.

176

In obedience, the dog is required to go into a sit position when the handler comes to a halt. This need not be a problem in the conformation ring. It can be accomplished quite simply by teaching the dog the stand and stay commands first and the sit when stopping routine second. Thus, when you come to a halt in the conformation ring, either say "Stand" and "Stay," or give the hand signal for same and *voilà!* The dog will be in a very showy conformation pose.

Those people who do not understand obedience training usually complain that the dog's spirit is broken with obedience training. Nothing could be further from the truth. The same charisma that is desired in the conformation ring is also wanted in the obedience exercises. A dog that has a low level of confidence and spirit is not a good obedience performer.

While some of the foregoing obedience exercises may seem to be relatively easy, it must be remembered that the Chihuahua faces some unusual problems, primarily because of size. For example, in the Stand for Examination exercise, what may appear to be easy is in reality quite a feat, because the dog must accept handling by a complete stranger. To the tiny dog, this stranger appears as a looming hulk, perhaps as much as fifty times larger than the dog.

In the heeling exercises, the Chihuahua faces the coldness of drafts, dust from the floor and noise bouncing off ceilings at indoor shows. At outdoor events, the Chihuahua encounters obstacles of long grass, spiked weeds, holes in the ground, strong winds and pelting rain. Unlike competition in the conformation ring, where large tents are provided, the obedience Chihuahua must perform in all kinds of weather without protective tent covering.

More obstacles are encountered in the Open Class, where two of the exercises are conducted with the owner or handler out of the ring. These are the Long Sit and the Long Down, where the dogs are lined up in a row and given the command to sit/lie down in the "Stay" position for three and five minutes respectively, while the handler leaves the ring and is out of sight of the dogs. For a little dog, this can be rather traumatic. A Chihuahua is quite emotionally attached to its owner, and for this reason sometimes finds this exercise a difficult one to learn. In addition, with less coat than many other breeds, the Chihuahua must lie down in cold and drafty areas. Outside he must contend with sharp grasses and little stones on the turf, plus heat, cold or rain.

The Tracking Dog title provides additional hardships, and thus not many Chihuahuas have achieved a TD. The obstacles are great:

weight of long line and harness, ability to scent not being a strong inherent trait, length of distance from handler, high grasses, potholes in fields and so on. Through all these difficulties, however, the Chihuahua, with a stout heart and great innate intelligence, has managed to achieve all obedience titles that are available.

For obedience competition, the exercises increase in difficulty for each progressive title to be earned under AKC rules.

Novice Classes, leading to a CD (Companion Dog title) include six exercises (quotes are from the AKC):

1. Heel on Lead and Figure 8 are to test "the ability of the dog and handler to work as a team."
2. Stand for Examination requires that the dog must "stand in position before and during the examination and that the dog display neither shyness nor resentment."
3. Heel Free shows how the dog and handler continue to work as a team but now there must be absolute control, for the dog is no longer on lead and must obey the handler simply through voice or signal commands.
4. Recall has the handler leave the dog in a sitting position at the far end of the ring. The dog must stay put until the vocal command or signal is given to come. The dog must respond quickly and come directly to a sit position in front of the handler; then upon command, the dog will end up in the heel position.

   The four exercises described above are performed individually.
5. The Long Sit is done with a group of dogs and handlers. The dog remains in a sit-stay position for one minute with the handler at the far end of the ring. When the handler returns, the dog must remain in sitting position until released by command, when the handler returns to the dog's side.
6. The Long Down is somewhat similar in that the dog must remain in the down position, with the handler at the other end of the ring, for three minutes and must remain down when the handler returns until the handler gives the release command.

Open Classes: Three qualifying scores in these classes, under three different judges, is required as in the Novice Classes, to earn a CDX (Companion Dog Excellent) title for your Chihuahua. Once this title is earned, the dog may continue to compete here, but only

Brite Star Orion, CD, a Dog World award winner, tied for first at the AKC Centennial Show in Philadelphia. Here he demonstrates a good return following the **Retrieve on the Flat,** an *Open* exercise. Owned by Elizabeth Bickel.   *Terry*

Glaisdaleast Fantasia, CDX, easily clearing the **Broad Jump**, an *Open* exercise. She held a top obedience ranking for five consecutive years. Owned by Elizabeth Bickel.

in the Open B Class. Open A is reserved for less experienced dogs and handlers.

The seven exercises comprising the Open Class are:

1. Heel Free and Figure 8, as in Novice Classes, require the dog and handler to work as a team. This exercise is more difficult, as it is done entirely off lead.
2. Drop on Recall is somewhat similar to the Novice Recall, but differs in that, partway into the recall, the dog must drop to a lying-down position upon command and remain down until the handler calls the dog to come once again.
3. Retrieve on the Flat, is an exercise in which, upon command, the dog retrieves an object in the shape of a dumbbell, made of a heavy hardwood or of a firm, nontoxic, non-wooden substance, excluding metal.
4. Retrieve over the High Jump requires that the handler throw the dumbbell over a high jump made of solid boards. Upon command to retrieve, the dog jumps the boards, picks up the dumbbell and carries it back over the high jump, returning the dumbbell to the handler. The jump is adjusted to the height of dog.
5. Broad Jump length is adjusted for the dog's height. The dog is left in a sitting position in front of the jump. The handler goes to the side of the jump, directs the dog to jump the boards and the dog does so and returns to sit in front of handler.
6. Long Sit is an exercise in which the dog must remain in a sitting position until the handler returns to the dog. The handler leaves the ring and remains out of sight for three minutes before returning to the dog.
7. Long Down is the same as Long Sit, but with the dog in the down position and the handler out of sight for five minutes.

The Long Sit and the Long Down are group exercises. The others are performed individually.

Utility Class: A dog earns a UD (Utility Dog) title upon completion of three qualifying scores under three different judges in either Utility A or Utility B Class. The B Class is for experienced dogs and handlers and also for continuing competition.

Utility exercises are six in number:

Okatoma's Mr. Cool, CDX, earned a CDX with a class placement for each leg. He has two legs toward his Utility title and practices the **Bar Jump** here, one of the Utility exercises. Breeder/owner is Patricia Lambert.

Ch. Rayal's Blanco Y Negro, UD, tries to combine the *Open* exercise **Retrieve over the High Jump** with the *Utility* **Bar Jump**.

1. Signal Exercise requires that the dog respond to stand, stay, drop, sit and come by signals only. The handler must not speak to the dog during this exercise.
2. Scent Discrimination, Article 1, shows five identical objects, each with a different number, not more than six inches long and made of rigid metal. The handler selects one and the remaining number are placed about twenty feet away. The handler places scent on the selected article by rubbing it. This scented article is placed among the others, while handler and dog face away from all articles. Upon turning to face articles, the handler simultaneously sends the dog to retrieve the scented article. The dog must return the scented article to the handler.
3. Scent Discrimination, Article 2: Same as above, but the objects are made of leather.
4. Directed Retrieve requires that, with dog and handler facing away from the far end of the ring, someone places three white cotton work gloves evenly spaced across the end of the ring. Handler and dog turn to face the gloves. Upon a signal from the handler, the dog is directed to retrieve the particular glove designated by the judge and return it to the handler.
5. Moving Stand and Examination asks the handler to command or signal the dog to heel and walk forward about ten feet. Upon order from the judge to "Stand your dog," the "handler, without pausing, commands and/or signals the dog to stand, continues forward" several feet and turns to face the dog. "The dog must stand and stay in position" where he is to accept the examination by the judge with no shyness or resentment. After completion of the examination, the handler calls the dog to the heel position.
6. Directed Jumping has the solid high jump at one side of the ring. At the other side is the striped bar jump. The dog is sent away from the handler and commanded to sit at least ten feet beyond the jumps. Upon a signal from the handler, the dog is directed to clear one of these jumps. The exercise is repeated for the other jump.

Tracking: A dog may earn a TD (Tracking Dog) title by going over a scented track between 440 to 500 yards in length. The track must be made by a stranger and be not less than half an hour old,

PRINCESS TERRY-JEAN, U.D.T.

Princess Terry-Jean, UDT, was the first Chihuahua to earn a Tracking title. She was owned by Rita Trench.
Drawing by E. R. Terry

184

Ch. Singletwin's Tiny, CD, finished with two five point majors and her CD on the same weekend. Handled by Trina Chicvara for owner Corrine Singleton.

Graham

Ch. Okatoma's Lickidy Split, CDX, finished his Championship at eight months, breeder/owner handled by Patricia Lambert. "Skeeter" has been High Scoring Toy in the top ten Obedience Chihuahuas and is a certified Therapy Dog.

nor more than two hours old. At the end of the track will be a glove or wallet, which must be found by the dog, who is on lead at all times.

Tracking Dog Excellent test: This title is abbreviated with the initials TDX. The scented track is not less than three nor more than five hours old and made by a stranger. The track layer will drop four dissimilar articles. The dog is to follow the track and either locate or retrieve each article. There are two judges for this, and the entire event may take more than one day. Each test is longer and includes more turns than the TD test.

A dog may become an Obedience Trial Champion, abbreviated by the initials OTCH, by earning a total of 100 points with a First or Second Place ribbon competing in the Open B or Utility Classes.

There are other classes for competition, but for which no titles are awarded. These are called Non-Regular Classes.

Graduate Novice Class is for those dogs that have earned a CD, but are not quite ready for the CDX or Open Class.

Brace Class is for two dogs of the same breed, to work in unison, performing the exercises of the Novice Class.

Veterans Class is for dogs eight years old and over who have an obedience title and are not entered in any regular class at the show. The Novice exercises are used.

Versatility Class is for dogs capable of performing all the exercises from the Utility Class, but who need not have a UD. There are six exercises; two from Novice Class, two from Open Class and two from Utility Class. There are no Group exercises. Exercises to be performed are determined by a draw of cards listing the exercises.

Team Class is for four dogs performing the Novice Class exercises simultaneously, except that the Drop on Recall is used, rather than the Straight Recall. Dogs in this class need not have obedience titles. This class has two judges.

All classes, regular and non-regular, have a minimum passing score.

The descriptions of what is expected in various aspects of obedience trials and tracking tests have been presented in the simplest form. For detailed explanations and rules pertaining to the exercises, write to the AKC for the pamphlet entitled *Obedience Regulations.*

Training a Chihuahua is not difficult if one uses common sense. Equipment must be light and reprimands must be gentle, but firm and consistent. Training sessions should be short. Ten to fifteen minutes at a time, once or twice a day, is all that is needed. These should be on various surfaces such as grass, carpet, wood floors, and

Am./Can. Ch. Terrymont Trifle Bit of Candy, Am./Can. CDX, won a five point major and was Highest Scoring in Obedience on the same day. Breeder, E. Ruth Terry. Owners, Herbert and E. Ruth Terry.
Kelly

cement, as one or more of these surfaces may be encountered in actual competition.

Beginning training should take place on familiar territory until the dog gains confidence, then switch to different locations. With new locations every few lessons, the dog learns to be attentive under all conditions and locations. You might even try a training session outside in light, misty rain. This is good preparation for outdoor Obedience Trials.

If the trainer does not have a strong back for continuous bending while beginning the early training for the sit, stand and down exercises, these can be taught with the dog on the grooming table. The dog will then have confidence at all heights, and the training can be used in both the Conformation and Obedience rings.

If you get angry, frustrated or tired, stop the training. It is better to train the dog while you are in the best of moods; the dog will learn much faster. The dog, too, must be in an alert and happy state.

Anytime you are having trouble training for an exercise, try getting down to the ground to see the jumps, the articles, the dumbbell or the gloves from the Chihuahua's perspective. It will help you in training and solving problems from the dog's eye level. For example, what you may see as two Broad Jump boards may only look like one big board to a Chihuahua.

Proceed slowly in the training. Many people rush to train the dog in the next exercise before the first one has been completely learned. However, there will come a time when the next exercise should be taught in order that the dog not become bored with going over the same routine, time after time. Vary the exercises. In heeling, do not always walk in a straight line. Try a left about turn, as well as a right about turn. This will keep the dog alert and make for better coordination between dog and handler. Try left and right circles. Mix up the exercises. Start with a different one each time. Learn the exercises at home first, so the dog will not have to "study" so hard in class.

You will find that Chihuahuas are individuals and will learn at different speeds—on some days, three steps forward and one backward. Just as in humans, there will be good days and there will be days of bad performance. Just take it slow and easy. You will have a wonderful time training and enjoying your Chihuahua.

Besides the Obedience Trials, take your Chihuahua to nursing homes and hospitals and show off your dog's newfound skills. The

Am./Can. Ch. Kitty's Kute Kupi, Am./Can. CDX, on the left. Am./Can. Ch. RJR's Kute Koy, Am./Can. CDX. Both owned by Evelyne White.

Ch. Brite Star Christmas Canis, CDX, Highest Scoring Dog in Trial winner for Elizabeth Bickel.

189

Judy's Wendy Robin, UD, earned the title at age eight. Owned by Judith Dickhaus.

patients will love it, and will be amazed that these little ones can perform so well, with skill and intelligence. Needless to say, you will be proud of your Chihuahuas.

CHIHUAHUAS WITH UTILITY DOG (UD) TITLES

Backman's Hot Chocolate, UD
Backman's Quate Nino, UD
Barnell's Cricket, UD
Chilton's Midnight, UD
Cris's Tiny Tinker Belle, UD
Edens' Prinsetta-Patsy, UD
Kayser's Pinto, UD
Kelly's Little Man, UD
Little Imp of Thames, UD
Ch. Rayal's Blanco y Negro, UD
Rineacre's Judi K., UD
Rineacre's White Krismas, UD
Riney's Tiny Miss Keto, UD
Sparkle Boy, UD
Summers' El Zorro, UD
Ch. Summers' Little Black Sambo, UD
Teko of Donna Kasparek's, UD
Judy's Hap Happy, UD
Murray's Alexander the Great, UD
Judy's Wendy Robin, UD
McCasland's Diablo, UD
Gochenour's Clipper, UD
Judy's Beau Black, UD
Don Charlie, UD
My Spanish Princess, UD
Rineacre's Jolly Roger, UD
Ch. Lockhart's Georgia Skeater, UD
Ch. Terrymont Marsubri Totc Ruff, UD
Lady Bitsy, UD
Rineacre's Chocolate Fudge, UD
Margaret Reichenbach, UD
Wilkin's Duquesa Cinderella, UD
Jasper Wildwood Robin Ruff, UD
Blaisdell's Annie Laurie, UD

Can. OTCH My Spanish Princess, Am. UD. Owned by Susan Fischer Payne.

Am./Can. Ch. Terrymont Marsubri Totc Ruff, Am./Can. UD. Bred by Terrymont Kennels and Marcia Greenburg. Owner, Susan Fischer Payne.
Ashbey

Ch. Summers Little Black Sambo, UD.
Owner is Laura Summers.

Wilkin's Duquesa Cinderella, UD, is owned
by Josephine Wilkin.

193

Tito Tequilla A Go Go, UD
Glad Rags, UD
Wilkin's Duque De Cassini, UD
El Pequena's Sundance, UD
Hewitt's Shelley Shabel, UD

CHIHUAHUAS WITH TRACKING DOG (TD) TITLES

Gin-Ed's El Poco Toro, CDX, TD
Mipi's Rushin Fizzgig, CD, TD
Gin-Ed's Miss Lisa Francis, CDX, TD

CHIHUAHUAS WITH UTILITY DOG TRACKING (UDT) TITLES

Princess Terry-Jean, UDT
Banda of Red Oaks Corner, UDT

18

The Chihuahua as
a Working Dog

MOST PEOPLE WOULD go into hysterical laughter upon mentioning the Chihuahua as a "working" dog. They immediately think of "working" as herding sheep, guarding cattle, protecting the house and so on. Working, however, can mean many other things.

Chihuahuas work as dogs for the deaf. Chihuahuas work as participants in therapy for the handicapped and those confined to nursing homes. Chihuahuas work as prison dogs and in other rehabilitation programs. Chihuahuas can be trained to excel as trackers, and can easily be used as drug locaters, for they can get to areas where larger dogs cannot go. Chihuahuas are outstanding guardians of the home. They excel as performers in show business. In other words, Chihuahuas can and do work and make a valuable contribution in many areas.

HEARING EAR DOGS

Chihuahuas play an important role in our society as dogs for the hearing impaired. As a hearing dog a properly trained Chihuahua alerts the owner to the telephone or doorbell, the baby crying, the tea kettle whistling, or the stove and oven timers. A Chihuahua can signal if the smoke alarm sounds and awaken an owner when the alarm clock goes off or if someone in the house is sick. For deaf automobile drivers, Chihuahuas can be trained to alert drivers about emergency sirens. Size becomes an advantage, for they can be taken anywhere, and readily adapt to small quarters.

In addition to special hearing dog training, such Chihuahuas are well versed in obedience training, for they must respond and quickly alert their deaf masters to what is happening.

I quote from a letter from Mrs. Robin Dickson, the executive director of Dogs for the Deaf, Inc., Jacksonville, Oregon:

> We have used many Chihuahuas . . . in our program. Their size and energetic temperament make them well suited for the work of a Hearing Ear Dog. Chihuahuas are ideal for older recipients who live in apartments or small houses. We have Radar in New York; Huey in Oroville, California; Snooka in Portland, Oregon, and Nacho who was in Hood River, Oregon.
>
> Nacho was one of our real "hearos." She was a little Chihuahua . . . who was placed with an elderly couple. One night she frantically woke the husband, and he got up and started to follow her out of the bedroom. At the door going out of the bedroom, with Nacho in front of him, he was confronted by a man wearing a ski mask and carrying a long knife. Nacho began barking and trying to protect her master. The intruder panicked, reached down, slashed Nacho's throat, and then fled with his two accomplices. Tragically, Nacho died, but we truly feel she sacrificed her life to save the lives and property of her deaf master and mistress. For her bravery, Nacho was given the Stillman Award by the American Humane Association.

Sheila O'Brien, the executive director for the Hearing Ear Dog program in West Boylston, Massachusetts, says that they, too, have trained Chihuahuas in their program for the hearing impaired. One was Chico, who was owned by Jean Cohen. They are currently training a dog named Peanut. These Chihuahuas and other similarly trained dogs look like any other pet, but they can be recognized by a brightly colored collar, leash or tag.

Owners go into training, as well as their dogs, in these programs. Some of the training is at the institution's facilities and some in the new owner's home. It usually takes three to five months to train a hearing dog. Owners learn how to care for the dog, including simple first aid. There is standard basic obedience training using verbal and hand signals.

Chico, a dog trained in the "Hearing Ear Program," did a marvelous job for his deaf owner, Jean Cohen. Chico completed his "sound training" in four months and performed his duties faithfully and expertly. Chico, an abandoned Chihuahua, was rescued by the local humane society and subsequently trained at the New England Educational Center Hearing Ear Dog Program in West Boylston, Mass.

The prospective recipient of a hearing dog must be old enough to provide full and responsible care for the animal. The yard must be fenced in, or at least provide an enclosed run of suitable size for the dog. Physical and medical care must be available. The hearing dog must be the only dog in the household.

The American Humane Association has several training centers for dogs to fill this vital role in society, in addition to those mentioned above.

THE HUMAN-ANIMAL BOND

Centuries ago, only the wealthy or those of royal blood could own a dog or two. In today's society, wealth has little bearing on pet ownership. Close relationships between people and dogs have been going on for centuries. Current research and behavioral studies between humans and dogs have produced some very interesting results.

It has been shown that children with dogs or other pets relate more kindly to other animals and human beings and show more responsibility in society. Pets help children and adults during traumatic times. Many times our stress can be relieved or blood pressure lowered by talking to and stroking our pets. Having a Chihuahua in a lap cuddling up to a human will bring forth smiles and provide comfort.

Dogs can be of immense emotional value when there is a death in the family. Caring for a pet during this unhappy period can help a person to muddle through the bereavement. A dog helps a person feel needed. They help us display our inherent need to care and nuture. Dogs are loving companions, playmates and protectors. A Chihuahua can keep one from being lonely and can raise emotional spirits. Chihuahua size is cuddly size.

Although a dog or other pet plays a greatly positive role in early childhood, the child must be of an age to readily accept the responsibility of owning a pet. In the case of a Chihuahua, there must be the ability to handle it with loving and gentle care. As much as a child wants to play with a Chihuahua, it must be understood that the small size requires an extra-special gentleness. The Chihuahua must have nap times as well as playtimes, and the child should learn not to pester the dog while the dog is eating or sleeping. Most children and adults consider the dog to be a member of the family, to be included in most activities.

The responsibilities of caring for a pet give a child a feeling of independence, self-confidence and sharing, as well as accomplishment. For adults, research shows having a dog will alleviate stress and hypertension, and will increase longevity for those who have had heart attacks.

A dog can provide activities for those who are retired or widowed. Knowing that a dog needs grooming, feeding and exercise keeps one active and gets the person out of the house for some human exercise. Someone who stays in the house constantly can easily become depressed. A dog keeps one socially aware. When out for a walk, it is not unusual for a stranger to strike up a conversation with you about your dog.

Playing with a dog helps to prevent people from focusing on loneliness, depression and unhappiness. Keeping busy with a dog means less time to dwell on problems in our own lives. For many a lonely person, a dog is his only companion and family member.

For the person living alone, the Chihuahua is much more than a lap dog. In today's society, Chihuahuas are useful in many areas. One area in which they excel is as watchdogs. This is especially good for the person living alone. Chihuahuas have extremely acute hearing, capable of recognizing the slightest sound from a possible intruder. The high-pitched sound of the Chihuahua bark, creating quite a din, can be enough to alarm the single dweller. This bark is loud enough and constant enough to ward off an intruder. It is the noise rather than the size of the dog that makes them so good at preventing intrusion.

THERAPY DOGS

There are kennel clubs, obedience clubs and other organizations that specialize in the use of therapy dogs. Members of these volunteer groups take their Chihuahuas and other breeds to visit patients and residents of nursing homes, hospitals and senior centers.

It has been well established that visits to these institutions do much for these folks. The loving, caressing and patting of the animals provides a release from tension and loneliness, bringing smiles to faces and lifting the spirits.

Through research, the Delta Society of Renton, Washington, has played a leading role in establishing the value of the human-animal bond. To quote from the Society's literature:

> The Delta Society began in the 1970's in the minds of a small group of sensitive professionals, people who recognized the importance of animals as companions. Research indicates that companion animals

Ch. Okatoma's Sergeant First Class, also known as "Trooper," enjoys the Pet Therapy programs. Trooper is well known as the elf in local Christmas parades. He is breeder/owned by Patricia Lambert.

Ch. Terrymont Pnut Brittle Ruff and Ch. Terryway's Tootsie Roll Kid give and receive love through the Pet Therapy Program, as seen by the pleasure on the faces of these seniors. Pnut was bred by Terrymont Kennels and is owned by Mrs. Juan DeLara. Tootsie Roll is owned by Terrymont Kennels and was bred by Mary Ann Minervino.

have a profound effect on the mental and physical health of people. Animals are being used successfully in therapy with emotionally disturbed children, adult patients in mental hospitals, prisoners, and the aged in chronic care institutions. Pets positively influence the physical health of their owners. Companion animals can reduce stress and have been shown to increase a patient's chances of surviving a serious illness. Pets offer something to love, touch, exercise and laugh with.

Dogs, especially, play an important role in a patient's ability to communicate with another living creature. There are some uncommunicative patients who will speak only to the dogs and utter not a word to another human being.

Man's best friend can also be man's best medicine. Research shows that animals and humans interacting seems to provide some sort of healing power, both mentally and physically. When properly matched, the human and the animal pet can go a long way toward a life of mutually satisfactory mental and physical stability.

SCHOOL PROGRAMS

Besides providing emotional and physical therapy for those confined to medical facilities or other institutions, many kennel club and obedience club volunteers take their Chihuahuas and other canine charges to local schools. These are educational as well as enjoyable exchanges for the young pupils. Instruction is given in grooming, feeding and general care of dogs as pets, as well as simple instruction in obedience training. Pet responsibility is stressed highly in these programs. The youngsters are encouraged to participate, with a question and answer period and actual demonstrations of how to approach a dog and stroke a dog with love and gentle care.

A typical Pet Responsibility Program lasts about 45 minutes and includes the following:

Proper grooming equipment for different dogs	How to pick up a small dog
How to groom	Provisions for food, water, shelter
How and when to bathe	Simple training techniques
Care of ears, eyes, teeth and nail cutting	Exercising
Veterinary checkups and immunization	Playing with and displaying affection for one's dog

Mrs. Lorus Gemmer, age ninety-three, mother of Millie Williams, gets a little love from Will O'Wisp Lil Fanciful Pin-up, two months old.

A one-hundred-year-old patient enjoys patting Ch. Terrymont Pnut Brittle Ruff, while two Borzoi owned by Fred and Carol Vogel look on.   *Terry*

203

Above all, the children are taught that we do for dogs because they cannot do for themselves and because we love our faithful companion pets.

A fitting conclusion to this chapter is provided by the stories of two heroes:

Peppy, the Hero

This is a poem written by Ruth G. Bahlman, co-owner with Rose Mioduszewski of RJR Kennels in Baltimore, Maryland. It is an account of a real event, occurring at the home of May and Bill Sutcliffe. The intruder was apprehended.

> 'Twas a Saturday night and at the Sutcliffe's house
> A creature was stirring, and it wasn't a mouse.
> While May and Bill were snug in their bed,
> Their Chihuahua named Peppy was using his head.
> He held his head high and sniffed the night air,
> There was someone at the porch door who shouldn't be there.
> Swiftly, yet quietly up the stairs Peppy did take,
> He whined and he cried until Bill did awake.
> Bill knew something was wrong when he heard Peppy's alarm,
> He motioned to May to keep Peppy from harm.
> Bill listened, and hearing the snipping of screen,
> He hurried downstairs where an intruder was seen.
> Bill cried, "Halt or I'll shoot!" as he held his hand out,
> The intruder turned, startled, then quickly he ran, when he heard Bill's shout.
> There's more to this story, it's needless to say,
> But Peppy's the hero who saved the day.

Rudy Toot, Hero

Another Chihuahua hero was Champion Florin's Rudy Toot, who saved the life of his owner, Nellie Florin.

While alone in the house with Rudy, Mrs. Florin prepared some food and placed it in her oven. While it was baking, she went into another room, where she fell asleep.

Some time elapsed, when she was awakened by Rudy, who was pawing at her arms and face. Upon awakening, Mrs. Florin discovered that the house was filled with smoke. She was able to get to the telephone to call for help and escape through the front door, while waiting for the fire department. When help arrived, Mrs. Florin had to be hospitalized, and Rudy was taken to the veterinarian for medical care.

It was a happy ending. Both survived the ordeal because of the early warning by Rudy Toot, Chihuahua hero!

Oliver North, a young Long Coat owned by Brenda Brewer, finds a new definition to the word "travel" as he works out on the treadmill.

19

Have Dogs—Will Travel

IF YOU OPT to travel with your pet, whether you are exhibiting, visiting with friends or relatives, or on vacation, there are special requirements. First, make certain that your pet is in good health. If you are crossing the border into another country there will be additional requirements, such as health papers, rabies certificate, vaccination papers and proof of ownership. If exhibiting, other documents may be required. Each country has its own requirements. Check with the appropriate consulate, area kennel club where exhibiting or local humane societies.

Make certain that pets are allowed at your motel. *Touring with Towser* is available from Gaines Food Products, for a small fee. This will list all the hotels, inns and motels that accept pets. Individual hotels also have booklets that describe these requirements. They may be obtained free of charge from most establishments.

Providing the motel will accept pets, the pet should be confined to a carrier of some sort, so there is no chance of soiling the furnishings while in the motel room. Pets that are housebroken in their own environment, frequently are not when taken to a strange place. This is because they have a tendency to mark the territory with their own scents, establishing a turf, so to speak.

If you are planning to visit relatives or friends, be certain to tell them you are traveling with your pet. The friends may be allergic or they may not like animals.

Your pet should be wearing a license tag at all times during traveling. It is even better if the dog has been tattooed and registered with a national organization that will have a record of the pet's tattoo number.

Pets that travel should be well trained in simple obedience, particularly to the come-when-called command. Pets are prone to jumping out of cars when least expected and getting away in a flash. Training a dog to respond to the word "come" will be of immense value here. The dog's lead should be long enough for an exercising walk during travel time and while you are at the motel.

Take along some of the dog's toys. Include a favorite blanket and be sure you have food and drinking water with bowls for each of these. Taking along drinking water will avoid diarrhea. The travel carrier can be used as a bed in the motel.

Your dog should travel in some kind of a carrier for his protection and yours. A dog that is loose in the car can cause an accident by jumping onto your lap while you are driving, or may become injured if you have to apply the brakes suddenly. The carrier should be strapped down securely. Seat belts looped through the handle of the carrier will do the job.

Do not leave your dog in the car during the hot months of the year. You may have left your car under a tree where there is shade, with the windows open a little, but this is not sufficient to provide coolness. Even if the car is left in the shade, heat builds up very rapidly. In just a few minutes, your dog will suffer heat stroke and die. To avoid this, there are over-the-shoulder carriers that look very much like tote bags, but are constructed with air holes for ventilation. This will provide comfort for your dog while you are sightseeing.

If you must leave a dog in the car to accomplish a quick errand, be sure there is sufficient ventilation and the car doors are locked. Return to the car in ten minutes maximum.

Every time you stop, and every two hours is a good idea for both humans and dogs, take the dog out for exercise and to relieve himself. Give water, but no food. Feeding time should be at the end of the travel day.

If traveling by plane, some airlines will allow one small dog in a carrier that fits under the seat on each flight. Other airlines state that your dog must ride in the cargo hold. Be sure to find out if the cargo hold is pressurized and how low the temperature will go. The carrier must be large enough for the puppy to stand up in and must

A sturdy carrier particularly good in warm weather and approved for airline travel.

be leakproof. There must be sufficient ventilation and there should be some kind of exterior edging to prevent other baggage from cutting off the air circulation around the carrier. The carrier must have the owner's name and address, as well as the destination, name and address of the person to whom the dog is going. There should be a large sign marked LIVE ANIMAL, a THIS SIDE UP arrow and telephone numbers of people at points of departure and destination. The crate must be sturdy enough to prevent crushing.

There are travel agencies that specialize in arrangements for exhibitors who fly with their dogs to other countries.

If you are contemplating a vacation, or if you will be away for several days at a time on business, the best thing you can do for your pet is leave it at home. To do this, you may find a reliable pet-sitter to stay in your home. A part-time sitter who will visit your home several times during the day, let the dog out, feed and exercise him is also a possibility. Or, find a reliable boarding kennel.

It is by far better to leave your puppy in the home environment than to impose the stress of travel, or leave your pet in a motel room while you are sightseeing. Pets left at their own homes often have better appetites than those left in a boarding kennel. Extensive travel may also affect appetite.

Leaving a puppy in a boarding kennel, no matter how wonderful the sanitary and other conditions are, may lead to parasites, kennel cough and other ailments. There is no way of knowing how other owners who leave their dogs there take care of their pets.

The pet sitter must be absolutely reliable. You do not want your dog running away, with the sitter reluctant to search. The pet-sitter must certainly like animals and have a rapport with yours in particular. If the dog does not like the sitter and vice versa, you had better make other arrangements. The sitter should have some basic knowledge of dogs, so as to recognize when your pet may be ill or require veterinary care. Be certain to notify your veterinarian that you have a sitter, or that your dog is in a boarding kennel.

No matter where you leave your dog, have the establishment checked out thoroughly. Is it reliable? Get references. Is it kept clean? Choosing a boarding kennel is as important as choosing your veterinarian or family doctor. Look before you board. Be sure to talk to the owners of the boarding kennel, in addition to looking at the facilities. Do they really care about the animals being boarded?

Tell them about any special needs or requirements for your dog, such as heartworm medication. Look at where your dog will be kept, in an individual area or packed in with other dogs. Everything should be clean, neat and orderly. There should be someone in attendance around the clock. Be certain you understand the cost of everything. If you say "Give Fido a bath while I am gone," do not assume it is part of the boarding fee. Everything extra that you ask for will have an additional charge.

There are pamphlets available about boarding kennels from various organizations such as the American Boarding Kennel Association in Colorado Springs, Colorado, the Humane Society in Washington, D.C., and also from your local ASPCA.

A problem for pet owner and dog show exhibitor alike is how to locate dogs that are lost or stolen. This is particularly important when traveling in a foreign country. License tags or other name tags attached to a dog's collar are only of limited value, as these items can easily be removed by taking the collar off the dog.

The most common permanent means of identification for dogs is the tattoo, either in the ear or in the groin. Many European countries require that the dog be tattooed before it can be registered or shown. National tattoo registry organizations in the United States charge a small lifetime fee, for which an owner may register a dog's tattoo number. Tattooed dogs are rarely stolen.

The Canadian method of identification is the dog's noseprint. This is required for CKC registration.

There is now a new means of pet identification. This is a tiny microchip which is injected under the skin. The pet can then be identified using a scanner passed over the microchip. Those veterinarians using this method claim that the injection of the microchip is painless. This system is marketed by Infopet Identification and Recovery System in Los Angeles, California, and is available through veterinarians.

Many countries have featured Chihuahuas on their postage stamps.

20

Chihuahuas in the Arts and Hobby Collecting

ONE OF THE earliest known paintings that included a dog recognizable as a Chihuahua is located in the Sistine Chapel. Attributed to Sandro Botticelli (c. 1482), it is a fresco depicting the story of Moses. Included in this work are the head, legs and tail of a little smooth-coated dog with long nails, round head, and large eyes, being held by a male figure. This painting was executed at least ten years before Columbus made his first voyage to this continent. This makes the history of the Chihuahua even more mysterious.

Sir Edwin Landseer, in a work entitled *Diogenes,* painted a smooth-coated dog resembling a Chihuahua, standing near a King Charles Spaniel.

Toulouse-Lautrec, who painted many different kinds of animals, completed a work entitled *Lady with a Dog.* This shows a small, smooth-coated dog, very much like a Chihuahua, being held in the lap of a woman. This work is located in the National Gallery of Art, Washington, D.C.

In the late 1800s Chihuahuas were already in show business. Rosina V. Casselli, a British music hall performer, had a troupe of a dozen or so Chihuahuas performing various types of trick acts.

Xavier Cugat, noted Latin-American band leader of the thirties and forties. He was famous for carrying a Chihuahua while leading his band.

Terry

214

Billie Holiday, the renowned jazz singer, was the owner of a Chihuahua named Pepi.

Terry

215

Christine Ebersole, multitalented actress, comedienne, and singer, is a devoted Chihuahua owner. The dog's name is Margarita.
Terry

216

osh, the Kuvasz, performs with Terrymont assy Lady, a Long Coat Chihuahua puppy on the *Captain Kangaroo* TV show. Both re four and one-half months of age and wned by Terrymont Kennels.

Well-known artist Edward R. Klein displays his drawings and ceramic sculpture.

Miss Casselli was one of those who believed that the Chihuahua was originally a wild dog.

In more modern times, one of the most famous people owning and performing with Chihuahuas was the Latin American band leader Xavier Cugat. He was usually seen on stage holding one of his little dogs. Although he does not mention the Chihuahua specifically in his autobiography, *Rhumba Is My Life* (Didier Publishers, 1948), Cugat does provide an anecdote concerning his dog. He relates that when refused admission to a hotel in the Southwest because of his dog, he wrapped the dog in a blanket and put a bonnet on it, saying it was a baby and thereby obtaining a room. This would have had to be a tiny, Chihuahua-sized dog.

Another reference to the breed was in Cugat's financial ventures. He said he had a partnership interest in a company manufacturing the "Chiwawa shirt." Cugat, also a noted illustrator, showed many Chihuahuas in his pictorial characterizations.

A well-known actress/singer/comedienne of the 1980s, Christine Ebersole, is a Chihuahua fancier. Ms. Ebersole frequently brings her Chihuahua, Margarita, to work with her.

Billie Holiday, the noted jazz singer, was also a Chihuahua owner.

Some of our Chihuahua breeders have made the rounds of the late-night television talk shows with their performing dogs. Jane Sewell, then of Gardena and now of Canoga Park, California, appeared with Barnell's Cricket, a tiny Smooth Coat with quite a large repertory of tricks and costumes. Linda Glenn of Harrington Park, New Jersey, appeared on late night TV with Sampsen, also a Smooth Coat.

The author has appeared on the "Captain Kangaroo" television show with a Chihuahua and a large white Hungarian dog, the Kuvasz, at the same time. In addition, several of her Chihuahuas were in print advertising.

Herman W. Schloo, of Vista, California, has a wonderful group of six Chihuahuas that are highly skilled in all sorts of trick acts.

Shirley L. Dear, from British Columbia, Canada, is noted for her performing Chihuahuas.

Chihuahuas have been used in advertising, photographic art shows, movies and PBS television. Episode #5 of the PBS show "Cats and Dogs" has a ten-minute spot featuring the author with a Long Coat and a Smooth Coat Chihuahua.

Barnell's Cricket was a regular performer in show business.

Louise Van Der Meid

Stand and be counted. From the left, Sparkle Plenty, Lita, Minx, Numy and Poco. Owned and trained by Herman Schloo.

Figurine collecting is a popular hobby. These are by Anita Chambers, United Kingdom.

Figurines by Alberta "Pat" Booth of Gardena, California.

A fine porcelain sculpture designed by Gunther Granget and made by Lorenz Hutschenreuther, Germany.

A pastel portrait of Ch. Kay's Don Feleciano-L, a well-known Long Coat Chihuahua of the 1980s. At the time of campaigning, the dog was owned by Kay Darrah. He is now owned by Ruth Morrow and Dick Dickerson. *Portrait by E. R. Terry*

Ch. Smithers' Lil' Indian Feathers, sire of twelve champions, owned by Ruth Morrow. Artist is Ce Ce Canaga.

221

Desde muchos años antes de la Conquista existió en México el perro pelón, al que se denominó XOLOITXCUINTLI y que fue compañero inseparable de los Nahuas (Aztecas) y Tarascos, tanto en vida de éstos, como después de su muerte. Lo atestigua la figura en barro ilustrada en este timbre, procedente de una tumba que data de hace más de mil años, descubierta en el Estado de Colima.

Stamp collecting featuring dogs is a fun hobby. This is a first-day cover of Aztec sculpture.

Translation: The hairless dog existed in Mexico many years before the Conquest. The Xoloitzcuintli was an inseparable companion to the Nahuas (Aztecs) and the Tarascos in life and even after death. Testifying to this relationship we see the clay figure depicted in this stamp, originating from a tomb over one thousand years old discovered in the State of Colima.

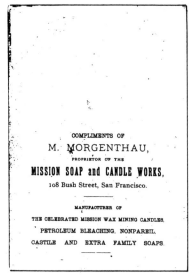

In the early part of the century merchants distributed advertising cards similar to the baseball cards that are traded today. This one appears to be of a Chihuahua.

The most recent movie featuring a Chihuahua as one of the main characters is *Oliver and Company,* a full-length animated film from the Disney Studio, released at the end of 1988.

On the stage, the road company of *Anything Goes,* in 1988/ 1989, featured a Smooth Coat Chihuahua bred by Elinor Hastings, Poughkeepsie, New York, and trained by Bill Berloni, noted animal trainer for show business.

COLLECTIBLES

There are many kinds of collecting hobbies associated with Chihuahuas that are fun and yet inexpensive. One of these is collecting Chihuahua figurines. Many of these can be found easily in the United States. Some outstanding ones have been obtained from British and German artists. Others are portraits for personal wall hangings, and for greeting cards and letterheads.

Stamp collecting is a great hobby. It takes you to other lands, tells stories, depicts history. It is an especially enjoyable hobby when it is joined with breeding dogs, Chihuahuas in particular. Chihuahuas are portrayed on stamps from many faraway and unusual places that are not normally associated with the breed.

A photographic portrait of Best in Show and Specialty winner Ch. Bliss Hoosier Boy Named Sue. Only the fourth Long Coat in history to win an all-breed Best in Show, he is also a second-generation Long Coat Best in Show winner.   *Paulette*

21

Chihuahua Clubs
in the United States

THE CHIHUAHUA CLUB OF AMERICA was founded in the state of New York in 1923, by a few people who were dedicated breeders and fanciers. The Queensboro Kennel Club in New York was the site of its first Specialty show, in 1928. The Specialty show and corresponding Annual Meeting were moved to Chicago in the mid-1930s.

While early progress was slow, moving the club to a central location did wonders for both club membership and popularity of the breed. Since that time the club membership has grown considerably and thousands of Chihuahuas are born every year. The breed has become increasingly popular in all aspects of exhibition.

In the beginning, usually one Specialty show was held each year, occasionally two. In April 1977, a second and rotating Specialty show was added as a permanent event, to be held in the spring of the year. The first of these was hosted by the Chihuahua Club of Atlanta. The author was privileged to judge this event, at which more than 150 Chihuahuas were entered. The author also had the honor of judging the Long Coat Chihuahua entry at the Fiftieth Anniversary Specialty Show held in Chicago in 1973.

Originally, Long Coats and Smooth Coats were shown together. Then, in 1952, the American Kennel Club, with the Chihuahua Club of America's sanction, approved separation of the breed into two varieties for show purposes. This may have been an additional impetus for gaining popularity. Soon after, the breed increased dramatically in litter registration and in the number of dogs exhibited. For many years now, the Chihuahua has been in the top twenty most popular breeds among all breeds recognized by the AKC, and in the top five for all Toy breeds.

The Chihuahua Club of America is the Parent club for all regional Chihuahua Specialty Clubs. All matters pertaining to Chihuahuas must be approved first by the Parent club, before going to the AKC for approval. The Chihuahua Club of America is responsible for maintaining the Standard for the breed and for insuring that this Standard is adhered to and promoted by all members.

From the humble beginning of a handful of people, today's Chihuahua Club of America boasts a membership of over 300. Across the United States there are several regional clubs. Names and addresses of the local secretaries may be obtained from the AKC. This is the current listing of regional Chihuahua clubs that are approved by the Chihuahua Club of America.

Chihuahua Club of Alabama
Chihuahua Club of Greater Phoenix (Arizona)
Southern California Chihuahua Club
Chihuahua Club of Northern California
Tampa Bay Chihuahua Club (Florida)
Chihuahua Club of Atlanta (Georgia)
Las Vegas Chihuahua Club (Nevada)
Chihuahua Club of Maryland
Chihuahua Club of Michigan
Chihuahua Club of Mid-Jersey (New Jersey)
Chihuahua Club of Greater New York (formerly Chihuahua
    Club of Metropolitan New York)
Chihuahua Club of Oklahoma
Nashville Chihuahua Club (Tennessee)
Dallas Chihuahua Club (Texas)
Houston Chihuahua Club (Texas)
Texas Chihuahua Club
Evergreen Chihuahua Club (Washington State)
Chihuahua Club of Greater Milwaukee (Wisconsin)

Each of these regional clubs holds its own Specialty show. Sometimes they are independently held shows, and other times they are held in conjunction with an All-Breed Show, on the same grounds and on the same date.

With an independently held Specialty show, there is a Best of Variety awarded to each coat. These two winners go on to compete for Best of Breed and Best of Opposite Sex to Best of Breed.

When Specialty shows are held in conjunction with an All-Breed Show, only Bests of Variety are awarded to the two coats. There is no Best of Breed award. That is because both varieties of Chihuahuas must be represented in the Toy Group. If a Best of Breed were awarded, it would mean that one of the Varieties was defeated, making it ineligible for the Toy Group.

In addition to the Specialty shows where points are awarded toward the dogs' championships, the regional clubs also put on Specialty matches, where dogs and exhibitors can practice handling techniques. Wins at these events do not count and no points are awarded toward championships. These matches are wonderful places to learn, for dogs and humans alike.

References

Basic Guide to Canine Nutrition, edited by James H. Sokolowski, D.V.M., Ph.D., and Anthony M. Fletcher, D.V.M. Chicago: Gaines Pet Foods Corp., 1987.

The Canine—A Veterinary Aid in Anatomical Transparencies, with Supplemental Color Illustrations. Grafton, Wis.: Fromm Laboratories, 1967.

Canine Pediatrics—Development, Neonatal and Congenital Diseases, by M. W. Fox, B. Vet. Med., M.R.C.V.S. Springfield, Ill.: Charles C. Thomas, 1966.

Canine Terminology, by Harold R. Spira. New York: Howell Book House, 1982.

The Chihuahua, by Anna Katherine Nicholas, Neptune City, N.J.: T.F.H. Publications, 1988.

Chihuahua Guide, by Hilary Harmar. London: The Pet Library, 1968.

The Collins Guide to Dog Nutrition, by Donald R. Collins, D.V.M. New York: Howell Book House, 1972.

The Complete Chihuahua, by James Watson, Anna B. Vinyard, Rosina Casselli, Milo G. Denlinger, and Rev. Russell E. Kauffman. New York: Howell Book House, 1978.

The Complete Dog Book, Official Publication of the American Kennel Club. New York: Howell Book House, 1984.

Dog Anatomy—Illustrated, by Robert F. Way, V.M.D., M.S. Croton-on-Hudson, N.Y.: Dreenan Press, 1974.

Dog Locomotion and Gait Analysis, by Curtis M. Brown. Wheat Ridge, Col.: Hoflin Publishing, 1986.

The Dog—Structure and Movement, by R. H. Smythe, M.R.C.V.S. New York: Arco Publishing Co., 1970.

The Dynamics of Canine Gait—A Study of Motion, by Leon Hollenbeck. Fairfax, Va.: Denlinger's Publishing, 1981.

The Mating and Whelping of Dogs, by Captain R. Portman Graham, L.D.S., R.C.S. (Eng.). London: Popular Dogs Publishing Co., 1961.

The New Dogsteps, by Rachel Page Elliott. New York: Howell Book House, 1984.

Pet Chihuahua, by Tressa E. Thurmer. Fond du Lac, Wis.: All Pets Books, 1962.

The Popular Chihuahua, by Thelma Gray. London: Popular Dogs Publishing Co., 1961.

Small Animal Medical Diagnosis, edited by Michael D. Lorenz, B.S., D.V.M., and Larry M. Cornelius, D.V.M., Ph.D. Philadelphia: J. B. Lippincott Co., 1987.

This Is the Chihuahua, by Maxwell Riddle. Neptune City, N.J.: T.F.H. Publications, 1959.

Who's Who in Chihuahuas—Volume I, by S. M. Dick Dickerson. Privately printed by the author, 1979.

ISBN 0-87605-125-5